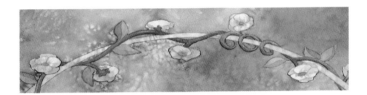

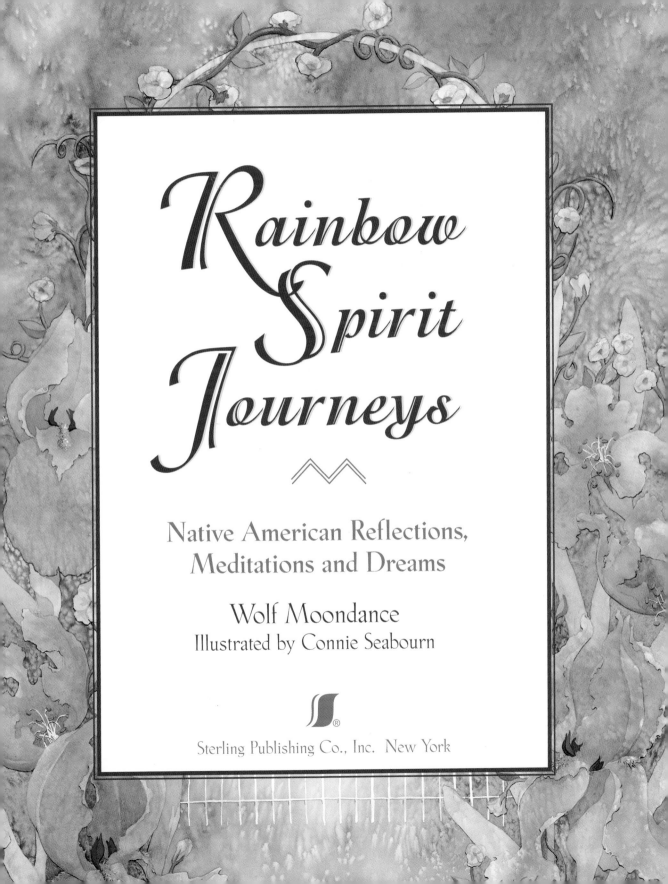

Rainbow Spirit Journeys

Native American Reflections, Meditations and Dreams

Wolf Moondance

Illustrated by Connie Seabourn

Sterling Publishing Co., Inc. New York

To Joe—
I had a dream and it came true.
I had a vision and it was you!
XO—Always

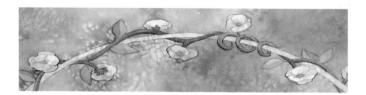

Library of Congress Cataloging-in-Publication Data
Moondance, Wolf.
Rainbow spirit journeys : Native American meditations & dreams / Wolf Moondance ;
illustrator, Connie Seabourn.
p. cm.
Includes index.
ISBN 0-8069-0563-8
1. Spiritual life. 2. Indians of North America–Religion–Miscellanea. I. Title
BL624.M6624 2000
299'.74-dc21   99-044619
1 3 5 7 9 10 8 6 4 2

Published by Sterling Publishing Company, Inc.
387 Park Avenue South, New York, N.Y. 10016
Text copyright © 2000 by Wolf Moondance
Illustrations copyright © 2000 by Connie Seabourn

Distributed in Canada by Sterling Publishing
℅ Canadian Manda Group, One Atlantic Avenue, Suite 105
Toronto, Ontario, Canada M6K 3E7
Distributed in Great Britain and Europe by Cassell PLC
Wellington House, 125 Strand, London WC2R 0BB, England
Distributed in Australia by Capricorn Link (Australia) Pty Ltd.
P.O. Box 6651, Baulkham Hills, Business Centre, NSW 2153, Australia
Printed in China

Sterling ISBN 0-8069-0563-8

$\mathcal{A}$CKNOWLEDGMENTS

$\mathcal{I}$ would like to acknowledge and give my heartfelt appreciation to a group of wonderful students who stepped out of the mist and walked out on that mountain, who walked through that East gate and looked from the spirit world to the pretend world from 1989 to 1992. I think each one of you will know who you are. The list is long and we counted coup, didn't we? We watched the red flag, the orange flag, the yellow flag, the green flag, the blue flag, the purple flag and the burgundy flag take flight along with your visions. I acknowledge you for staying with me during that time and each of you remembers the soft twinkling of the lights in the Medicine Wheel those evenings when Ceremony was our intention. I thank you for believing in me, and you are as Real as I am Real, as reflections of the spirit world.

I would also like to acknowledge a Native singer, Butch. I will always have memories of you bringing up your heritage in yourself and singing your heritage. May the wind always find its way through your lungs and may your words always be eagle spirit.

I think that the acknowledgment page in *Rainbow Spirit Journeys* is simply me wanting to reach out to each of you—each of you who read the book, each of you who have studied with me, each of you who have supported me in your belief over the years of my walk on this earth. It's me giving, through my Creativity, spirit journeys for each of us to find reflections of the spirit world in our lives, and I want to acknowledge that here in this wonderful opportunity and work.

I usually just say thank you to Sheila Anne Barry, but I want to give you a big hug and say what a delight it has been. We have spent precious time together from 1992 till now. Soon we will start our eighth year, and with us, there is no time and no years—just birth of the works. Like I said one time, you have felt like a mom to me and I want you to know, and I want your family and your grandchildren to know, what a wonderful editor, person, friend, student, creator you are. My BIG XOXOXO to you, Sheila Anne Barry.

And I usually just breeze through and say thank you, Granny Jo, for your magical fingers. I acknowledge you for walking in one evening and pushing your way onto a list by believing that was the class you wanted to take, becoming a student, asking me to push ahead always and bring more to life. And it doesn't matter, does it, what I write—you're going to keep asking for more. This year you have asked me to write children's stories for your grandchildren and I'll have to say yes, and I do say yes. I say thank you for the children and thank you for the grandchildren, and for theirs to come, seven generations, that they might hear the word of Great Spirit through Rainbow writings. Joanne, Granny Jo, Dancing Spirit, thank you for being that perpetual student and asking, and for your magical fingers that type these words, correct them, and argue about them, because that makes it fun.

Thanks to Joe—your love guides and warms my heart!

And my gratitude and much love to my half-side Raven for giving me support and a life of true spirit journey.

Aho.

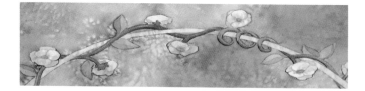

CONTENTS

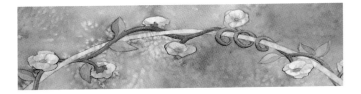

INTRODUCTION

When I was very young I heard the wind blow, and I followed it. It was always blowing ahead of me, and I followed it out the back door, through the flower garden, into the orchard. Wind spirits surrounded me and began to talk. One of them spoke to me, and said, "Look in front of you and you will see a path." I can still hear that voice today, so clear. And around that spirit voice swirled the soft sounds of the wind—singing, chanting, whistling, conversing. "See that path? Follow it." I can feel myself walking on the hot dirt that was that path. "Follow me," I heard a sweet voice say, and I did. Into a land beyond the smells of the flower garden, into the sky, beyond the sun, within the stars, beyond the Rainbow Bridge, beyond the Milky Way, on the other side of the moon—way out there.

To know spirit, you must understand spirit. To understand spirit is the gift of spirit. To tell others about spirit is a true gift. I am a mixed blood, Native American and English. I draw on both worlds. I walk, live, and teach shamanism. Sometimes my soul cries out for "the good old days," and then I remember my Grandma saying to me, "Don't long for the good old days, for these are the good old days." Now, my Grandma Lil wasn't an ordinary person. She was French Cajun, and she adopted me when I was ten. She was a unique lady and she taught me a lot about the spirit world and journeying. She taught me, when I wanted to drift off and even die—like a lot of young people do in their teen years—to go beyond life and let go of the physical. She listened to my story about the wind spirits, and she agreed that I should follow the path. As I went on and became a teacher of spirituality, I guided many students in spiritual matters and allowed them to open their hearts to spirit and hear Great Spirit, Grandfather, Creator, God.

Her voice often rings in my mind, in her teaching about journeying. Within this book I will lead you on guided reflections of the spirit world. They are Native American in that they deal with the elements and spirits, spirit teachings, and the spirit world. They are a gift that was given to me through my mom's blood, for my mom was very big, when I was little, on

taking me to the spirit world. She would allow me to walk from the earth up into the sky and beyond, to the teachers who waited there to show me the things that Great Spirit, Grandmother/Grandfather wanted me to bring to earth to the two-legged. A lot of people say that my mom opened up my imagination, and I had a vivid imagination. I was taught that imagination is a small, limited space where you learn to fantasize, but when you step past that, through journey, you enter the land of the spirit.

I was also warned to be careful not to let go of my body, unless I wanted to live forever as a spirit. So I ask you not to let go of your body unless you want to go. Often in this life as a two-legged on the earth, we think we want to die, and that we would much rather live in the spirit world, because it is a place that is comfortable and we feel safe there. Let me say to you, as many teachers have told me when I visited the spirit world, that the earth is a good thing. It is our mother, and it has given us our two-legged experience of coming to school and learning the teachings of Great Spirit, and of all those who want to teach us in the physical form.

This book of journeys has been prepared for you to expand your spiritual mind, for you to meet spirit guides and see colors of energy in their purest spiritual sense. I will do my best to guide you in a spiritual experience in each page of this book. It is often very hard to take a journey when you are reading, so I suggest that you just relax and let all of your fears, all of your "knowledge" and all of your limited thoughts be free. Sit in a comfortable place where you won't be disturbed, or lie in your bed where you are warm and safe.

When you start reading a journey I suggest you take a journal with you—a notebook in which you can write down things that you have seen, felt, and heard, for you are truly stepping beyond your imagination into the spirit world. Keep your spirit journal so you can remember and experience and expand. I have often said to my students that everything is of the mind, and I would like to repeat that now, in the instructions of this book. Think of anything that didn't come from the mind. We step into the spirit world and bring things back, and make them happen. That is how materialization happens in my belief. Be careful not to bring things back from the spirit world to the earth and make them happen, because that way you are limiting them and holding them captive. Do not be selfish and greedy, do not covet and bring things back from there that are not yours. Everything is thought. Everything is energy. Matter is pure resonance of energy and form. When you go within these journeys, go to find the wisdom from the teachers.

Sit quietly when you start your journey. Breathe in through your nose, and out through your mouth. Take deep breaths, in and out—four to seven times, and relax, and continue breathing. Read the words and journey in your thoughts. You might want to take a tape recorder and read from the book, and then listen and follow along. I suggest that once you have read the journey, you can remember it and allow yourself to "go." "Going" is a term I use to separate you from limited material and place you in free spirit. It is always nice to journey in sunlight. It's wonderful to journey in a hot tub—you can float among the stars, in mists of color. Relax and journey.

When you go on the journeys, you will change. You will find a freedom and friendship connection to the greatness of the Great Spirit far beyond anything you have ever experienced. That is why I have never been a drug addict or an alcoholic or been dependent on liquor, gambling, or sex. That is why I am allowed to experience all things in life without bondage, entrapment, or being enslaved, for I can journey at any moment. Breathe in and out, relax, and before you, you'll see a familiar path....

When you are journeying, remember that everything is thought. A lot of things that you see, you'll feel you're making up. You'll feel they are not real. That is because of your limited mind—or because of the teachings of people who try to make you feel guilty. Jesus often spoke of the healings that came to pass, and he said, "...even greater things can you do." I believe he meant that we can have all that is ours from the spirit to the physical. And I truly believe that God is all things. I truly believe that Great Spirit, Grandfather, is all things. I truly believe that Grandfather/Grandmother, Great Spirit, is flesh and blood and bone. And as I journey into the spirit world, I know that flesh and blood and bone is not evil. I know that as we go within the lower world, into the depth of our despair and agony—we bring back our fears. As our mind journeys in its insanity, as it journeys in its weakness and its foulness, it gathers what it finds and brings to life evil. For evil is fear of the unknown. I know that there is no horned devil, nor has there ever been one in physical form, other than in our thoughts—and I know that it is limitations and our hysteria that make hell seem a reality. Everything in life is a spiritual journey (a thought). What we know of our spiritual purpose (good, uplifting purpose, and goals) is what we will have in our present life. Our spirit voice speaks with symbols—visions, day-dreams, nightmares, colors, and pictures in our mind. When we journey to understand our spirit voice, we can feel safe, warm and complete. We can allow our spirit journeys to guide our present walk in life, if we journal and interpret our spirit messages. Remember, if you have experienced evil and fear in your life, it will imprint your spirit and reflect in your journey.

As you journey in the spirit world, you will find that there is nothing but beauty and peace within Great Spirit, Grandfather/Grandmother, and that we are that creation. It is my hope that, as you use this book, each journey will lift you into the fullness of your rainbow self, so that you can open your heart into the sacred four directions, and live as a rainbow medicine wheel.

Journey work is prayer. It is meditation, daydreaming, and night dreams. But the difference is that in journeying you find out the truth about your needs, and answers to your dreams. You allow the spirit elders (ancestors) to guide your pathways in life.

CHAPTER ONE

SPIRITUAL JOURNEYING

ourneys are interesting experiences that I have used since the wind
spirit came to me. When we journey we allow ourselves to walk out of
our physical existence through our minds into the purity of our spiritual
bodies, and move about within spirit. The journey is a natural energy flow—not
a forced or premeditated action.

Let's look at the place of journey between the physical and the spiritual
world. In the physical world it is known as a trip, a tour, an excursion, or a
jaunt. It can be a ride, a drive, or a walk or run. There are cruises and voyages,
migrations, and emigration. Spiritual journey work is a pilgrimage, for a pilgrimage is going to a sacred or holy place. Frequently, a journey gets confused
with meditation. Meditations can be many things—mulling over, dwelling on ,
chewing over, being lost in thought, thinking of nothing, focusing on, wonder-
ing about, considering. And a journey can be a meditation, in that there is
studying, examining, reflecting, deliberating, or theorizing. Because the part of
the meditation that is spiritual goes on within a spiritual journey.

The purpose of a spiritual journey is to give you insight into the world of
spirit. Your thinking is spiritual; it is the voice of Great Spirit, Grandmother/
Grandfather. There is a difference between dreams, meditation, visions, and
journeys. A dream is the cleansing process of the mind, where it files and
processes all wanted and unwanted thoughts. Many times, in dreams, you
experience a premonition, which is your brain actually figuring out your future
by looking at the scenarios around your life. The brain is capable of putting
forth premonitions, strong warnings that the path you are on should be altered.

Meditation is also a clearing of the mind. It is allowing the mind a no-think
process, so that you are able to focus and have clear thoughts. During meditation you are to clear all thoughts from your mind and have an absolutely
thought-free consciousness.

A vision is a frozen journey. It is a message. It is something that stands still and takes on the form of a picture. It can be similar to a premonition in that it is clear and precise. But a vision is often like the picture on a book cover. It is a simple frozen thought that appears from a journey, which is the movement of spirit within your thoughts. Your vision is there as a road sign, a guiding picture that allows you to know that you have been given a message to interpret from Great Spirit, Grandmother/Grandfather. A vision can be seen as a picture map that shows signs to guide you in daily life.

Journeying is going on the path of thought. You are actually thinking into a pathway that takes you to the spirit world. This world has an upper realm, a middle realm, and a lower realm. The middle realm is the world you are at— where you live your daily life. In a journey, your thought patterns combine the lives and teachings of people who live in middle reality, the lives of those who live in upper reality, and the lives of those who live in lower reality. In upper reality you are brought guidance and conversations with Great Spirit, Grandmother/Grandfather, and also other ancient spiritual elders who bring about teaching. The message of the upper world is to remember that everything is a teaching. In the lower world, things are distorted, confusing, ugly, fearful, evil, and it is a place where turbulence and fantasy exist. It is a place of learning. When your mind takes you on a journey to the lower world, then you are challenged with the lessons of life.

When you look at four different dimensions—dreams, meditation, vision, and journey—then you have broken apart your ability to walk the path of thought. Interpretation is a very large part of spiritual journey. It is the ability to look at what you have seen, heard, smelled, or felt within the journey, and to apply it to your daily life.

I am going to stay within the realm of my own vision, and my own experiences, because I feel it is important not to steal another's medicine or another's power. When I learn something, it comes to me through the voices of my stars, and my stars are my spiritual guides. They are guides of my mind, and they teach me to live with Confidence and Truth, to leave my everyday physical world and travel past imagination and fantasy by journeying into spirit.

It is important to understand that there is a difference between spirit and the spirit world, and to know the difference between a spiritual place and the spirit world. Spirit can walk among us in the physical world, but we cannot walk in a physical form in the spirit world. A spiritual place is a physical place where you feel warm, safe, and welcome — a place where you can interact with the spirit of Self or the spirit world. It all happens in the mind through thought.

My life holds within it over twenty years of teaching spirituality in different ways, as well as Christian religion and philosophy, and lots of times I feel that as human beings we limit ourselves by separating from Great Spirit's energy in our mind—and feeling that we as humans are alienated. The way I have been raised, with my vision and my mother's teachings, I am not alienated from Great Spirit.

A journey is the opportunity to see Great Spirit's will, to have a mental picture of the will of Creator, Great Spirit, God. I often go into the realm of the spirit, which makes my belief shamanism. Shamanism is living in two worlds—the physical and the spiritual—being able to walk back and forth and hold on and maintain my identity. My identity is brought into form as your identity is brought into form, through spiritual guidance, spiritual application, spiritual development, and spiritual expansion. So I can say that within the Native American circle, everything is Great Spirit, all things are God—to be understood and to be respected as is all spirit.

So what is the difference between physical and spirit? Touching with the hand and touching with the thought. It's like the difference between water and vapor. It is very hard to touch a vapor. You have to really think about it to feel the mist on your skin. You can feel the temperature changes if the vapors are hot, but lots of times vapor cannot be touched with the skin. Whereas, water can be touched. It is that way with journey and meditation. I like to say a journey is a reflection—it is reflecting. So is there a difference between fantasy and journey and meditation? A fantasy is constructed by previous thought—that's how I like to define it. Which means that you take a situation and make it what you want it to be. In a fantasy, you make believe. You lie to yourself to make life the way you want it. In a fantasy, if people are fat, you just imagine them skinny. However, you don't expect your scenario to be God's will.

Journey is where we walk within the very core and existence of energy, resonance, vibration, frequency, spirit of — anything.

Within the place of journey, you receive guidance, understanding, and become peaceful and calm. You journal your vision journey and start to make sense of your message and set goals from the experience. A fantasy is made up of thought, the way your teachings in life take you or the life you tell yourself you need.

When we are working with fantasy we are limited by what we remember. I challenge each one of you to look at your fantasies and see whether they are things as you would like them to be, or things you remember, that you have seen in a picture, or in a word picture that someone has painted in your mind.

I offer the teachings of spiritual journeys for you to experience a rainbow—a rainbow being the very existence of energy that resonates into physical form. I was arguing with a teacher once about the spiritual and the physical. I said, "Well, there is no way physical can be spiritual, because you can touch it." He looked at me and smiled, and said, "Touch it in thought."

You can only touch in mind; the brain controls your nerve endings and records the reactions you have. Without the thought of touch, you cannot touch.

Now you think about that. Is the physical really as concrete as we would like to make it? Or is it only a thought resonating through extensive vibration? Well, in my years of shamanism and spiritual work, encountering apparitions and spiritual beings, I have come to realize that everything that we know as material is a thought. And it resonates at a frequency higher or lower—depending on what it is—and we can touch it simply through our thinking. Remember his message: Shut your mind off and you will touch no more. If you are thinking of a part of the body, and it is bumped or bruised, is swollen or has tumors, it won't touch anymore, and you won't feel. Matter, as far as I am concerned, is a physical realm that gives us the opportunity for a part of the brain to touch and a part of the brain to know.

Walking between two worlds is simply bringing thought into the resonance of memory, bringing thought into a spiritual picture. Now that may get a little complex. Take time and look at it. Feel it. Would you be able to know an apple from a ball, or from an orange, if you had no sight? In my training to become a shaman I was taught to go and expand my journey. I have a personal relationship with spirit—all spirit. For to me, Great Spirit, all of your prophets, Jesus, little things that go bump in the night, color, children and you—are all the same. For God is all things. It is my desire to teach you, through journey work, that you have control over your thoughts. That is your spirit mind. And that is God's will. In the Native circle we call God Great Spirit, because it is the grandest and the greatest point of all existence, the mystery beyond the mysteries; God does not separate from you. You are not less than it. The difference between Great Spirit and you is the difference between blue and pink. In understanding that, you must understand that you are not separated from Great Spirit. You are eagle, you are Great Spirit, you are tall tree, you are great wind, you are God in resonant forms of Self.

When I journey, and when I take you on a journey, there is a need for sacredness. The place where you journey must be quiet and you must be undisturbed.

So there must be respect from all for what you do. You must believe what you do; you must understand what I have said previously, and understand what you are doing. You are walking your spirit path, reaching in for your fullness and bringing it back. Often shamanism, spiritual journey, and things that have to do with the depth of spirit, are looked at as mumbo jumbo or trivial mind gems, fantasy, or imagination. One of my pet peeves in life is when a parent tells a child, "Oh, you just imagined that." There is no such thing as imagination in the world of the shaman. Imagination is simply a cop-out for not being able to experience or accept Great Spirit's wholeness. The world of the spirit is filled with all types of journeys, messages, and visions.

An interesting topic some people bring up is evil. Oh, the bad spirits, the evil spirits, the horned one, the one with the long tail and hooved feet. Think about the devil for a minute. It has horns. So do animals. Therefore, someone saw an animal's horn in the woods and conjured a thought of evil. It has hooved feet. So do many animals have hooves. A lot of them have split hooves, for they have two toes. "Oh, well that's evil." No. That's someone looking out in the woods and finding a way to deal with a fear of the dark, instead of understanding that it is a deeper shade of blue, or a deeper shade of green, purple, or burgundy, or a mixture of those—simply an absence of sunlight.

It is easy to declare an unknown fear is evil. We, as humans, can be so scared of the unknown that we will place blame on anything to explain our fear. That is why journeys can be filled with scary and blameful thoughts. Truth is a solid knowing, with the answer within it. Journey symbols are clear and bring answers to our mind's eye.

In shamanism, the world of journey that you are entering into in this book, if you bring an evil spirit into form in your spiritual journey, it is your fear. It is your desire to be scared. It is brought about by a teaching, and you can usually pinpoint it. You can take yourself back into your two-legged walk and you can go right to the place where you were taught to be afraid. It is someone's creative output that makes a monster happen. And I'm not going to tell you that in the journeys that I guide you through, I won't put you in places where you can look at your fears. For I will.

This chapter of instruction is for you and me to get to know each other better, for you to understand where I come from and how I teach. If you want your journey to be to the land of Jerusalem where Jesus lived, then you can go there and see that in your spirit walk. But you will be imagining, for you will be trying to put a teaching on top of an experience. Let yourself go when you journey.

When you meditate, you reflect. When you journey, you travel. So you actually go to your reflection.

What is the reflection? Is it a memory? Lots of times you think you have spiritual experiences, but all they are is something someone put in your mind to control you. Study history and you will see that government, people, covens, and cults are truly religions, are truly dogmatic, dictatorial directions from others' thoughts, to control and usually to gain financial power. It is much simpler when you step into shamanism, for you walk in the world of the spirit and it is pure. I call these Rainbow Spirit Journeys, because they open up an array of vibrational frequencies that bring about color, so that you can actually feel the energy resonating in the tones. This is the purest knowledge there is. Enhance yourself by reading all the books and articles on color that you can, when you study journeying. You need dream dictionaries, other dictionaries, studies of people who have written, for they have captured thoughts, as I do as a writer.

Captured thoughts are a good way to introduce the need for interpretation. When you have captured thoughts, you have a voice of spirit, and through your interpretation of its message you bring about an understanding of a journey, a vision, a dream, or a premonition. In meditation, interpretation is not necessary, for your mind is cleared. Interpretations are easy—don't try to make them harder than they are. When you are working with a spiritual journey, you are working with your own thoughts, your own needs, and your own pure consciousness. When you work with interpretation, there are lots of ways to go about it. You can allow someone else to interpret it for you, or look at other people's teachings and bring forth definitions that apply to your life—which means that you use dream dictionaries and their definitions of topics, as well as dictionaries that define words, as well as the charts in the back of this book, applying the interpretations guide to what you have seen. It is important to remember that you need to feel comfortable about your interpretation. If you have a spiritual journey, but you cannot make sense out of it, then you are closing your mind. You may be afraid, or perhaps you don't believe what has happened.

An interpretation of a journey could go as follows: I follow the path and there I see five beautiful trees. One of them is red, one is green, one is yellow, one is orange and one of them is dead. I return to my conscious state of mind. I bring about an interpretation of that by noting that I have seen *five*. Looking at the number guide in the back of the book, you will find that five represents the word "truth." So I know that these trees speak of truth to me.

When you are going on a spiritual journey, it is important to apply Intention to the journey before you leave. Intention simply gives your journey a subject matter or a title. If you go on a journey that has no Intention and no subject matter, then immediately the number will give you a key to what it is about.

Having seen a red tree, I go to the color interpretations, which tell me that the red tree speaks of my confidence, of strength, of nurture, of all colors, of being accountable, and that it is pure in spirit and brings me enlightenment. So I know that I am having a very strong, spiritual vision. I move on and I see a green tree, and I understand that the green tree speaks of all the green interpretations underneath the color headings. Likewise with the yellow and the orange. I move then to the fifth tree and I see that it is dead. It could bring panic to me, thinking that means my truth is dead. What I would have to do in those circumstances is to understand death. So I would turn to a dream dictionary, a regular word dictionary, a synonym book, and gather all the information I could on death, for it is speaking of my truth being dead. I would understand that my truth has left the physical plane and stepped into spirituality and that these five trees are my truth, that they are speaking about growth. The ongoing circle of life within a sacred circle is what the tree represents. Looking in the back of the book under the interpretation guide for plants, I see that one of the definitions of tree is "a cycle of life." Therefore, I know that this journey has taken me to a higher level of thinking that speaks to me with a statement that my truth has stepped into a spiritual realm, that it is going to bring forth a tremendous amount of growth, and open up opportunities.

It is fun to do interpretations because you can't go wrong. And yes, it is as big as you think. It is something that you can get excited about, something you can use to expand your life, and something you can use as a directional path to give you enlightenment and enjoyment. Sometimes in interpretations, I just simply listen. I interpret the five colored trees this way—that I am given five opportunities for growth. One of them might have to do with my red, one my green, one my orange and another my yellow.

The color scale has an order:

1 — red	4 — green	7 — burgundy
2 — orange	5 — blue	
3 — yellow	6 — purple	

I look at the order of the colors and I see that red is in the first position, green is in the second position, orange is in the third position and yellow is in the fourth position, with a dead tree in the fifth position. So that is like a period in a statement. I see a message in the fact that the colors are out of order. They tell me that I am to apply my red within my red, knowing that that is confidence, strength, etc. But in my Balance—my orange—I need to grow, I need to grow to bring it about. I need to have Beauty to bring about my Balance. I can apply all the words from the green to the orange.

In the third position I see that I have orange in my yellow, for orange is in the third position of color and yellow is in the fourth position of color in this journey. This allows me to know that my orange is speaking to my yellow, for it is in the position of yellow, and that my yellow is speaking to my green, for it is in the position of green. When you see colors out of order, they are telling you that you need to apply the color that you see to the position that it is in. Example: You need to apply green to your orange, because orange is a second-position color, and green is in the second position in your journey.

There are many ways to interpret your messages. Take your creativity and your mind and bring forth your own interpretations, because you can't go wrong. You must always remember that in a medicine wheel, in the sacred teachings in the mystery school, there is no wrong. When people bring fault, narrow-mindedness, guilt, or fear into spiritual work, they are confused and angry, bringing a negative influence to their own lives by choice.

When you are working with your journeys and nothing much is happening, just go on. Let your mind clear and you will walk into the path and you will begin to see. It is important to remember that if you see nothing to interpret in your journey, it is nothing. Nothing is a sign of emptiness or loneliness and a need for forgiveness and letting go, starting over. There is an interpretation for all things. So in physicality where we have to have a tangible sentence or a tangible structure, in a spiritual journey everything is up for grabs. It is open, it is able to be interpreted, it is able to be philosophically looked at, for it is the voice of thought, which is spiritual. It has no physical bounds and no physical limits.

Which brings us to the closing of this chapter, with a word called "journal." When we journal, we capture a thought and we hold it where our memory won't fail us. Thought becomes solid when we put thought into form, called writing. We think our writing becomes proper English as we say what we think. But we actually think it forth. I get tickled when people want to do spiritual work and they start to take off into it and then get confused and angry.

That is simply fear. A journal will help you not to be afraid.

Whatever your physical training in life—no matter what religion or race you are—you could be a skeptic. You could have feelings that you are not good enough, or that you don't belong in the spirit world. Everyone is always welcome in the spirit world, by Grandmother/Grandfather, Great Spirit. If you have any of those feelings, it is your consciousness trying to explain to you that you need to do a cleansing. That is simply done by clearing your mind of any wrongs that you have committed, and asking for forgiveness from Grandmother/Grandfather, Great Spirit. As you proceed, it is very important to let your mind just flow, looking at your thoughts as if they were a movie. If you should try to journey but have a hard time, sometimes it is physical. But most of the time it is because you need to just let your thoughts flow. I often describe spiritual journey as "I see," and I speak very clearly about seeing, but I also am able to smell and hear. We have all of our senses in our adventure of journeying into the spirit world. So in truth this sensing is simply what most call thought: you just need to let your mind flow.

THE STEPS OF SUCCESSFUL JOURNEYING AND APPLYING THE JOURNEY TO YOUR LIFE

1. Be sure you are in a comfortable place, a safe place, a place where your privacy is respected.

2. Make sure you are warm, or that you are cool enough, so that you are comfortable. Comfort is the step before relaxation, and relaxation is the step before letting loose, letting go.

3. The next thing you do is to make sure you have your journey notebook, diary, or tape recorder to catch your experiences, because they flit by fast.

4. The next step is to breathe and not be focused on any teaching or fear. For you are going to experience a spiritual trip.

5. Do not force it, but allow your mind to create. Do not make an image happen in your mind, for that would be fantasy or imagination. Just allow your mind to float, to be free-form, and travel-focused—looking, expecting. It is important in this step, when you are journeying, to expect and not to force. Forcing brings in a preconceived idea, while expecting is looking forward to the new.

6. Gather everything that you can when you journey, meaning, *think*. Remember *think*. Remember quickly. Hold on to it, bring it back and journal.

---

7. Next is coming back. Let go. Only take things in your thoughts that you are told to bring back. An ancestor spirit, a teacher spirit, a spirit on its own may say, "Bring this back with you." Only take what you are told to bring back. Never covet or hang on to any thoughts within journey.

8. The next step is coming back into physicality, where you will feel yourself actually moving into your body, for you are thinking yourself physical again. The breath of life, which is constant—the heartbreak of the earth, the pulsation of the ocean, the expansion of air—will keep you alive, for it is your will to breathe.

9. When you return, it is good to stop for just a moment and feel yourself. Think of your feet, your legs, your body becoming awake again in the fullness of your spirit entering into your body. Has your spirit left your body? No. It has expanded. Not disconnected, which is what "left" means. To leave is to disconnect. To expand is what you do when you journey. You allow your physical to release and allow you to go, which is an expansion of where you are. When you have returned and you have begun to feel yourself being solid, open your eyes wide. You'll notice sometimes you need to yawn. This is a balancing of chemicals within the physical brain itself. It is an actual combining of matter with resonant energy.

10. It's time to write down or speak into the tape recorder (I use a tape recorder because that's how I can get it down fast enough). For all of you with quick minds, get a tape recorder. Get everything down that you can from your journey. Begin to interpret your journey and list that in your journal. You do that by coming up with a complete rendition of what you just saw, felt, heard, smelled, and tasted. Bring it into realization. You can use the interpretation guides in the back of the book, along with dream dictionaries, dictionaries, encyclopedias, and other books that bring forth knowledge and help you apply the spiritual journey within your life. Construct your interpretation of what the journey means to you and how it sets forth a path for you to follow. Often your journey becomes your walk. It is so powerful, it is so wonderful, that there is nothing that can keep you away from the spirit of your existence.

11. The last movement of the journey is application. Remember that we dig our own holes. Remember that we put ourselves into debt by being lazy, by being hateful, by being afraid. There are many and various principles, variables in life, that cause us to separate into what we call "physical": Life is so boring, so mundane; people are so mean; those are all things that you want, those are things that you need in your life, because you have been taught those things.

And you will find within spiritual journey that you are free of these ideas, these limitations. So the last step is to obtain this freedom and bring it into form. It is easy to have a spiritual life if you think spiritual thoughts. Spiritual thoughts are praise, prayer, worship, duty, obedience, diligence, dedication, expectations, gratitude, and communication. These are all just words, unless they are put to work. Put them to work in thoughts and you have communicated shamanically. You have stepped through, brought something back, and made it a reality.

It is important to follow the journey instructions to come back immediately at the end of the closing. You are free to reenter any time you want but you need to keep your journey pure by not extending your stay. If you do try to stay, it moves you into the fantasy and imagination parts of your mind and you lose the pure connection of your journey. A spirit journey should last from three to fifteen minutes. When you are conducting a journey, it is a good idea to set a timer to call you back.

If you should hear your timer calling you back but you are not finished with your journey, come back immediately and journal where you have been and what you have done. Then reset your timer and enter again.

Spiritual journeying is done for your expansion of knowledge and direction within life. It is not something to be pushed on other people, or to suggest that you know more than someone else. It is used to stabilize yourself and to give yourself a purpose in life, to understand your surroundings and your present intentions. Spiritual journeying can be the answer for many things, such as low self-esteem, addiction, disappointment, detachment, and a lack of understanding. Spiritual journeying should not replace therapy, counseling, or structured medical treatment dealing with depression and other mental illnesses. Journeying is an application to strengthen your spirit voice and bring about a healthy mind in your physical existence.

CHAPTER TWO

LEARNING JOURNEYS

earning journeys will allow you to walk within what we know as the medicine wheel. A medicine wheel may be a new concept to some of you; it may be an understanding that is very old and feels very comfortable. A medicine wheel is constructed in many ways by many different teachers. All medicine wheels are built in a circle. They are built with stones or objects that represent a place in time. The Rainbow Medicine Wheel has within it four directions, the stones of the outer circle, which are medicines, and a cross in the center going from North to South and East to West, which represents the spiritual road and the physical road. It is the medicine wheel I have brought forth to teach the form and information from my personal vision, given to me from Great Spirit, to help all people.

This journey allows you to walk within the medicine wheel in your mind's eye and see which stone speaks to you. The medicine wheel is known as a mystery school. You can take the wisdom from within the medicine wheel and apply it to your daily walk, and grow strong in your own existence.

Find a place where you are warm and safe or cool and comfortable. Have your journal and pen with you, or a tape recorder, and follow me.

JOURNEY OF THE MEDICINE WHEEL

Breathe in and out, taking deep breaths in, and breathing out gently. Relax and let your eyes fall closed. Continue breathing and feel the warmth and comfort of your body. With your spirit eyes look before you. You will begin to see a path. The path is very familiar and comfortable. Follow the path by walking very slowly and very directly, breathing in and out, and relaxing. You feel the sun shining on you; you can hear birds singing. You smell the smell of the rich earth and the warm grass blowing in a soft breeze. Before you, you see a grassy

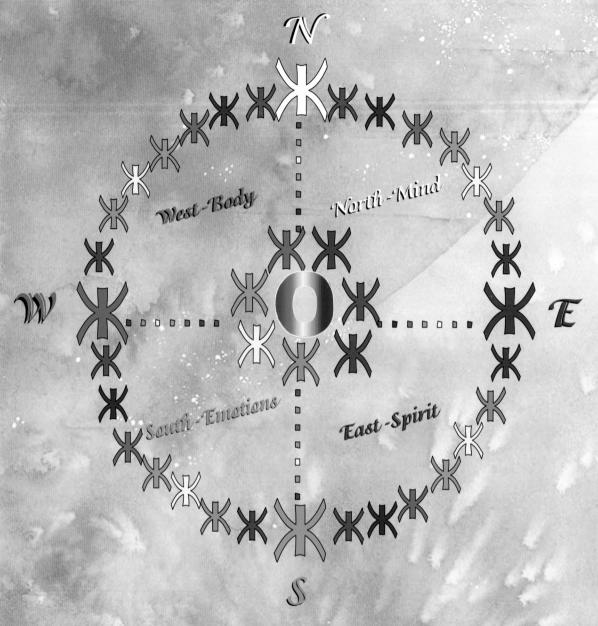

N

W

E

S

West - Body

North - Mind

South - Emotions

East - Spirit

Rainbow Medicine Wheel

START IN THE EAST
MOVE CLOCKWISE
MEDICINES ARE STARS
LESSONS ARE DOTS

area with stones that are placed in a circle. You recognize this area as a medicine wheel. You see the large stones that mark the four directions, and you see the sections of medicine in between the four stones that make a complete circle. You see a line of stones going from North to South. In the center is a stone with a circle around it. You see a line going from East to West made of stones. You listen very carefully. Pay attention to everything you hear. Record the sounds that you hear in your mind. Look around the wheel and see your message from the medicine wheel. Remember what you see and what you hear, to bring back and record in your journal.

You feel yourself coming back into your body, coming back to the warmth and comfort of yourself in the physical form. You open your eyes and remember what you have heard and seen in the medicine wheel. Remember if you saw any animals or colors in a certain area, or any spirits, or sounds. Remember what you have seen.

Open your journal and record the symbols, the sounds, the pictures and the information the medicine wheel has given you. When you have recorded your information, you are ready to interpret the messages that have come from the medicine wheel through your spiritual journey.

JOURNEY OF THE CREATOR AND THE SONG OF SPIRIT

You breathe in and out, softly and gently. You feel the connection between your physical self and your spirit. You feel warm and safe and comfortable inside your physical body. You breathe in and out, and relax. You continue breathing, knowing that you are going forth to communicate with the Creator and hear the song of spirit. The song of spirit is the Creator's voice. It may come in sight, smell, touch, or sound. Before you, it is very dark, and you feel yourself walking on the air. It is a wonderful feeling to walk on air. You walk out into the blackness, moving forward, and you come to a place where darkness becomes light, a bright-colored light. The Creator's message is in the color of the light, and you can see the color very clearly, for it is the ground that you would step on in front of you. You step on that color and you hear the song of the Creator. You listen very quietly to the sounds, or what the touch is, or what the smell is, or what you see. You remember everything about the song of the Creator. You feel the warmth, the coolness, the refreshing feelings of the song of the Creator. You thank the Creator for giving you this song, and you let go.

You feel yourself return to your physical existence, and you remember what you have seen and heard, smelled and tasted. Open your eyes and record in your journal what you have seen and heard, what you have felt. Record the color, the sounds, the objects that you saw, the critters, or rocks—anything that might have been there within the song of the Creator. You are ready to interpret the message of the Creator and the song of the spirit. This journey makes a strong connection between you and the Creator. It gives you a strong connection with the song of your spirit.

The medicines of life are your happy thoughts, objects that are sacred to you, people and animals you feel safe and have a bond with. The words of the Rainbow Medicine Wheel are:

Confidence
Balance
Creativity
Growth
Truth
Wisdom
Impeccability

JOURNEY OF THE MEDICINES OF LIFE

You breathe in and out, and relax. You feel yourself warm and comfortable within your physical self. You look before you and you see a path. This path leads you to the medicine wheel. You walk around the edge of the medicine stones that are the outer circle of the wheel. You see the big one and the little ones, the big one and the little ones, the big one and the little ones, the big one and the little ones, and the big one. You have returned to where you started. You have walked around the medicine stones. Now, as you continue to walk around the circle again, you will receive the messages the medicine stones wish for you to have. As you begin to walk around the stones, touch them—the ones that you should touch. There you will see your medicine. You will look at the stone and remember what number it is. You look at the color of the stone and

remember what color it is. You might hear a sound or see a shape—it may take on the form of a four-legged, a winged one or a crawly. Pay attention as you go around the circle to what stone speaks to you in the first section of the wheel, because it is about the spirit. In the second section of the wheel, it will be about the emotions. The third section of the wheel is about the body, and the fourth section is about the mind. Remember, within each section, what you have seen. Thank the medicine wheel for showing you these things that bring your medicines into position in your life. You hold this memory in your heart. You let go and feel yourself coming back to your body, where you are very warm and safe, very comfortable. You open your eyes, take out your journal, and record what you have seen in the medicine wheel: what you saw in the spirit section, in the emotion section, in the physical section, and in the mind section. Record what you saw, what you heard, what you felt, what you smelled. What you saw—such as colors, symbols, animals, people, objects—are the medicines that you need to interpret, to bring forth the message of the medicines of your journey.

This journey can be done to achieve an answer to any situation in your life.

JOURNEY OF THE LESSONS TO LEARN IN LIFE

Breathe in and out four times. Relax and allow yourself to be at peace, thinking no thoughts. You feel warm and comfortable, connected to your physical self. You let go. Before you, you see a path—a path that takes you to the medicine wheel. You begin to walk on the path. Listen, look, smell, and hear. You come to the wheel and you are facing the East rock. It is the section of the spirit. You walk within the wheel and you look at the lesson stones that make a line from East to West and North to South. You look at the lesson stones moving from the East to the center. Look at what you see—a stone, an object, a sound, a smell. You move to the South, to the West, and to the North sections of the lesson stones, looking very carefully each place you go, listening for each sound you hear. Which stone glows? What color do you see? What sound do you hear? What is there with you? What you see in each lesson stone? Bring that back in your mind, to write it in your journal. The East section of the wheel contains the stones of the spirit. Think of a stone from 1 to 7 in that section. The South section is the section of the emotions—think of a stone from there. The West is the section of the body. Think of a stone from the West. In the North is the section of the mind. Think of a stone from there.

There are seven stones in each path. Remember what number it was. Maybe there was more than one. Thank the lesson stones of the wheel, and let go. Return to the safety of your body, the familiarity of your warm physical existence.

Take your journal and record what you have seen and heard—what stone in what section, what noise with what stone, what color in what section—and begin to work on the interpretations of the journey you have taken to learn the lessons of life.

As you record the different journeys that you have taken, don't try to make sense of them—just write them down. Get complete notes of what you have felt and heard. Remember where you were in the medicine wheel, and what if felt like to be in the song of the spirit. Remember the medicine that was given to you, and the lessons you heard in the song. Write down everything that you have seen and felt, and then correlate it to where you were within your vision.

An example to help you: You saw bright colors; you felt soft breezes; and you were standing in the South. You interpret the color, and you know the soft breeze represents a beginning. The fact that it is a soft breeze means it is spirit. The spirit of the breeze is speaking to you of emotions, because it comes from the South. The color tells you the meaning of the lesson.

Then apply the teaching lessons to everything you do for the next seven days, seven weeks, or seven years. Everything is applied in ones, fours, and sevens—one day, one month, one year; or four days, four months, or four years; or seven days, seven months, or seven years. You set the time by stating to yourself that it will be one, four, or seven days or months or years. Remember, time is nonexistent in spirit, and the longest time spirit work can take is seven years in human form.

Journal everything that you have and then start to interpret. Have fun with it. Do not try to force it. Figure out how you can apply the message to your life.

CHAPTER THREE

SPIRIT JOURNEYS

Spirit journeys allow you to get to know the counsel of your spirit. Within the journeys that you take here, you will meet your spirit guides: the guide of your emotions, the guide of your body, the guide of your mind, the guide of your spirit. You will meet the spirit who guides and guards you on the earth. You will also meet your protecting spirit, which is your guardian spirit.

When you are working with spirits it is important to understand that you bring back in thought only what your spirit guide tells you. It can be a thought or a memory or an object. Record everything that you hear, smell, feel, and see. Everything around you, everything on the journey is a part of the message to be interpreted at the end.

Find a place where you are warm and safe, or cool and comfortable. Have your journal and pen with you, and follow me as I guide you on a Rainbow Spiritual Journey to meet the reflections of your spirit guides.

JOURNEY TO MEET YOUR SPIRIT GUIDES

You breathe in and out, and relax. Continue breathing easily, softly, in and out. Before you, you see a familiar path. This path leads you into the woods. As you walk along, you see high grass and trees all around you. In front of you a sunbeam is shining on a clear, round circle of grass. You step up to the edge of the trees, and you can see the clearing is very soft and peaceful. The soft ray is shining down, making the area very bright. You see seven standing together in a circle. These seven can take on colors; they can take on form as animals or winged ones; they can be sounds that you can recognize as an object; they can be plants or rocks, they can be anything.

The first one you look at is right in front of you. This is your spirit, the one standing right in front of you. Remember what you see, what you hear, what you feel, what you smell. Look at the subject very carefully, for you are looking at your spirit. Look at the color, listen for the sound.

Remember this, then move over to the left and look at the next spirit. The sun shines very clearly on it. Remember what color it is. Remember what it looks like. Remember what it sounds like, for this is the spirit of your emotions.

Move over to the left around the circle, and the sun is shining very clearly on the next spirit. It is very solid and you can see its personality. You can see its color. You can hear it. You are looking at the spirit of your body. Remember what you see.

Move left around the circle and standing there in the green grass is another spirit. Look very carefully at this subject. You can see it clearly. You can hear it. You can smell it. You are looking at the spirit of your mind.

You move around the circle to the left and you come to a spirit that is very strong. You can feel its presence and see what it is—what type of animal or two-legged, or what color the spirit might be is very clear to you. You are looking at the guide that protects and guides you on earth.

Move on around and you have almost completed the circle of spirits. The next one stands very strong You look at this spirit. You feel it, you hear it, you see it. This is the spirit that guides you in the spirit world. It is the one that you make contact with that allows you to go into the spirit world.

Move to the last spirit in the circle. Look at this final spirit and see what it is. You listen to it, hear how it sounds, sense how it feels to you in your mind. This is your protecting spirit. It is the one you use to protect you in all things that you do.

Step back now and look once again at your spirit guide, your emotional guide, your body guide, your mind guide, at the guide you use on earth, at your guide to the spirit world, and at your protecting spirit. Breathe in and out very softly, and remember who they are and what they are, how they sound and how they smell, what color they are. Thank them for being there. Begin to leave by walking through the woods. Turn and look; it is now very quiet in the circle, and the sun is no longer shining down.

As you walk away, feel yourself coming back to your body, the warm, familiar physical presence. You regain yourself, open your eyes, and work with your journal on what you have seen. If you have trouble with any of the spirit guides, you can return through the path to the clearing and call the spirits forth again, and walk through them to find the ones you are looking for.

JOURNEY TO SEE THE SPIRIT WORLD

Breathe in and out, and relax. Continue breathing and let your eyes close. You feel soft and rested. Let yourself drift into a deep state of relaxation, breathing in and out. Before you, you will see a path that you can walk on. This path is very familiar, friendly, and comfortable. It takes you to a place where you like to go. This is a place where you find peace and quiet, a place where you can relax, where nothing and no one interferes with your being. You feel warmth and quiet. At that place in your mind's journey, lie down and relax. You smell the sweet fragrance of flowers and spring rain. Breathe in and out, and before you, you see a stairway leading to the sky. The stairs go straight out in front of you— they do not go up or down, they go straight out like walking on a bridge. You begin to walk on that bridge of stairs. It is dark on both sides, and in front of you is a beautiful color. Remember that color.

You continue to walk until you step within the air of that color, until the mist of that color is all around you. Remember the color that you see, and the sounds that you hear. Remember what it smells like. You come to a place where you see the stairway is made of stars, and you can walk upward; you can walk high into the sky. You start to follow those stairs made of stars and you climb high. You step into a place where you can see clearly. It is unique to you, for it is your upper spirit world. Look at this place.

Look at the kind of ground it has, at the kind of sky it has. Look at everything. Each time you come to this place it is different, so see what you see now. Remember who and what you see, what it sounds like, what it smells like.

After you have been there for a while, come back down the stairway and remember what you have seen. Come back to the place where you stand, where it is misty and colorful. There you see a hole, with a ladder leading down. You go to the hole and start down the ladder. This will take you to your lower world. Climb down, deeper and deeper, and further down. What does it feel like? What does it smell like? What sounds do you hear? You come to a place where you can stop, and you are in the lower world. It is a place of unwanted thoughts, of lessons, and confusion. It is the place of fantasy. Look around and see what you can see, deep down below. Smell and remember. See and hear. This is a place where you can come to learn your lessons, to understand confusion, to look deep within your fantasies. Remember what you have seen and heard.

Climb back up the ladder, up to the place where you stand in the mist. Look

in front of you, and there is middle reality. That is the world as you know it. Walk out into what is so for you. When you step into your middle reality, you will be in your ordinary life. You will see things that are important to you, people who mean a lot, places that you like to go. Pay attention to what you see here, for this is important to your middle reality.

Come back into the place with the mist. Remember what you have seen in the upper world, in the middle realm, and in the lower world, for these are places in which you can gain advice, strength, and guidance. Look at your ordinary life, and think of your fantasies and lessons, to learn from the spirit world the things that you need to know.

Come back to yourself now, connecting with your ordinary life, remembering what you have seen in the spirit world. Bring it back to your journal and interpret and understand.

JOURNEY TO SEE YOUR SPIRITUAL ADVISOR

Breathe in and out, and relax. Continue breathing and relax. You will see a path in front of you that takes you along a lake. Follow the path. The lake is shimmering silver, for the full moon shines bright on it. There is a light fog around the edges of the lake. You walk to the edge and there is a stairway leading upward. It is made out of soft, silvery fog. Climb that stairway and walk into the sunlight of the spirit world, the upper world. You follow another path: it is red clay. You can smell the strong scent of earth. You walk among beautiful stones. Pay attention to the colors of these stones and what kind they are, for they speak to you of the medicine that your advisor gives you. The stones make a large circle and in the center stands your spiritual advisor. You look at this being and it can be anything. Give it form. It will take on its color, its smell, and its sounds. Listen to what your advisor has to say to you, what it gives you, what it shows you. Remember this. Bring back the wisdom that your advisor has given you, and the shapes and kinds of rocks that you have seen that are medicine. Put those things solidly in your mind to bring back to record and interpret in your journal.

You feel yourself coming back to your ordinary reality, coming into your warm and comfortable body. You take a deep breath and open your eyes. Record and interpret what your spiritual advisor has spoken to you about.

Journey to Awaken Your Spirit

Take a deep breath in, and relax. You feel connected and comfortable with your ordinary physicality. Breathe in deeply and let it out. Before you is a beautiful mist. Look with your spirit's eyes beyond the mist. Walk through the mist. You feel the soft, cool mist all around your body. You smell the earth and the rain.

There before you is a spirit being. The spirit takes on shape and form, symbols and smells that are familiar to you. Look very carefully at what the spirit is showing you. Step within what the spirit has shown you, and you become that. Walk forward on a little rocky walkway, and see before you a small trickling stream. Kneel down and look into the water. There you can see the spirit again. You have become your spirit. Reach down in the water and throw water over your head, and your spirit emerges clean and fresh. Look into the water and you can see your spirit. You may hear it or smell it; you may notice it as color, animal, winged one, or crawly. Remember what you see, for it is the awakening of your spirit.

Return to your ordinary self, reentering very comfortably, very quietly, very securely. Open your eyes, write in your journal and interpret what you have seen as the awakening of your spirit.

Spirit journeys are given to you to use any time you wish to work with your spirit guides, to see the spirit world, to find spirit advisors and listen to what they may have to say to you, or to awaken your spirit. At all times, these journeys will be light, clear, and clean. There will be spirits of clear thought, good thought, happiness. You will bring nothing back from the underworld—nothing from fantasy or confusion, nothing from mental torment or anything that will bring you any harm. Everything that you find here is to be used for the good of yourself and mankind.

CHAPTER FOUR

How Journeys Help your Spiritual Work

1. A spiritual journey brings about knowledge and helps you to know. That increases your Confidence. Your red medicine is Confidence. Medicine is a term that is applied to anything you use to bring about a good feeling, to bring about a good existence, to bring the good to life. Confidence brings Strength to your life. It opens doors to opportunity and success. When you take a spiritual journey, you expand your knowledge beyond things that you are told in a physical existence. You open yourself up to thinking for yourself.

For example, you see a moose in a journey. Your come back to interpret it and look up the definition for moose in the back of this book. You find that moose is mental, that it is about self-esteem, that it is the part of knowing that helps your mind to have its Strength and Confidence. This brings Confidence to your physicality and improves your self-esteem.

When you are using spiritual journeys to bring about a knowing, it helps to feel that you are in control of your life, instead of someone else telling you what to think. It is important, when you do your interpretations, to utilize all the definitions you can find that are given by all teachers for each thing that you see. Don't be strictly guided by one source, but look to many, for knowledge is vast and has lots of avenues. When you have this creativity within your avenues, it brings forth your Confidence in a strong way.

2. Understanding the spirit world gives you balance. Balance is an orange medicine. It allows you to obtain high energy. It allows you to expand yourself in both light and dark. It gives you the ability to be a two-sided individual—front and back, up and down—walking in total balance. When you understand through journeys, you understand your spiritual knowledge. No one impresses upon you their own beliefs. No one brings about your belief except yourself. When you understand the spirit world, you have a great understanding that balances you.

For example, you have a very keen and sharp personality. You are keen-sighted, sharp-thinking, and clear-minded. In a spirit journey you see your spirit brought forth as an eagle. It brings sense to your personality, in that you have keen eyesight and are very quick.

When you explore the spirit world through spiritual journeys and bring about an understanding that is strong to you in a personal way, this gives you Balance medicine, which increases the orange in your rainbow.

3. To experience a spiritual journey will open you up to Creativity. Creativity is yellow medicine. It allows you to expand and have options. When you walk within a spiritual journey, and are able to see, to smell, to hear, to feel—you have opened up the world of Creativity within your thought. You think you're standing still, but when you have a thought, it is vast. That vastness is your Creativity.

For example, you go on a spiritual journey within the spirit world and there you are shown words that have feet and hands and they run all over. You gather those words up and put them in a basket. Someone walks down the trail and you hand him or her a word. This spiritual journey has given you permission to teach. You are a teacher, who passes out words and knowledge. You bring the vision back and you interpret "words." They are the sharing of thoughts. You interpret the word "basket"—a place to gather, a place to hold, and the basket has held words, so it has held thoughts. It is a place where you share and hold thoughts, and you have given those words away out of the basket so you are in the place and you are the giver of thoughts. Therefore, you are a teacher, you are someone who expands other people's minds and words.

When you experience a spiritual journey, your Creativity is unlocked. It is open and expanding, and you have the ability to be whatever it is you wish to be. You are not set in stone. You are no longer bound within limits, but you are able to set goals and go forth in your Creativity.

4. To follow your spiritual journey will be Growth. Growth is a green medicine. It is a medicine that is often connected with pain or fear—for Growth is the unknown. It takes you into areas that you cannot control. It is the outcome of your desire. It leads to doorways where you find opportunity. When you follow spiritual journeys, they take you to places where you are given the answers. Answers are Growth.

Example: You are on a spiritual journey that takes you to a ring of flames. Sparks jump out and the ground catches fire. This journey has shown you that your energy cannot be contained, that it will jump and spread, and that movement is Growth.

Growth cannot be contained or kept. It is constant, perpetual motion. Through following your spiritual journeys, you are given the opportunity to understand that while Growth may appear to be scary, it is a natural flow. Growth is a green medicine. It is necessary to achieve it and to be well rounded.

5. In a spiritual journey you will expand your personal Truth in every way. When you feel the color, and you hear sounds, when you feel the wind as wings passing you, when you smell the campfires and the ocean, the mist of spirit, the force of color—it cannot be explained in any other way, except to say that it is your personal Truth. Holding on to the wisdom of what you have seen, and making sense of it in your interpretation, may take hard work, but Truth will expand your heart and your mind, in every way in your life. Truth is your blue medicine. It is solid with an expansion.

6. To apply what you experience in your journey to your life will bring about much Wisdom for your self-esteem. Wisdom is purple medicine. It is given to you from the voice of Truth. When you go into a spiritual journey and you see, for example, a black and white horse running in the night, and you feel yourself riding on the black and white horse, you become very quiet and still. You find the next morning that you fell asleep riding the black and white horse. Do not limit what you have seen, but expand on the Wisdom, realizing that you gained good rest that night, for the horse has carried you in spirit, where you found much peace and relaxation. Wisdom is the doorway to self-esteem. From knowing and bringing forth in your spiritual journey you can apply peace of mind to your everyday life. From that you have the self-worth to go forward, for you have permission within yourself to be strong.

7. To enjoy and feel joy from a spiritual journey will bring Impeccability to your daily walk. Each of us strives to be accepted, to be good enough, and to find honor and respect in our lives. When we go into a spiritual journey, we are often given pleasant thoughts.

Example: The walls were crystal clear and there were many bubbles. They floated around me, bouncing—peach-colored, lavender, ones of rainbows spinning and turning. The air was fresh and clear and I could breathe and find peace within myself. Within that vision I experienced pure child joy: I played with the feeling of floating, I held hands with color and relaxation. It brought about a feeling of absolute freedom and joy which was Impeccable.

I take that Impeccability into my daily walk and bring it forth as a knowing that our lives are not meant to be filled with anguish and despair, and we do not need chemicals to reach the realm of spirituality. We need only the quietness of our breath and the guidance of our teachers, our ancestors, and elders to achieve Impeccability in our daily walk.

Each time you take a spiritual journey in this book, allow yourself to think for yourself. Allow yourself to interpret, using other people's definitions, what your possibilities, potential, excitement, and stability are going to be. When you have a personal relationship with the spirit world, with its advisors, teachers, and guides, you build personal relationships that allow you to perceive life in a joyful way.

CHAPTER FIVE

Money Journeys

These are material journeys, journeys to help you understand material wealth. Luck (good luck) is a pathway to material wealth. Prospering, prosperity, and manifestation are all movements within these journeys that lie ahead. When you look into monetary gain, my advice is to strengthen your spirit and understand your physicality. Set goals and understand the avenues it takes to apply your Creativity and Strength to obtain material wealth.

Find a place where you are warm and safe, or cool and comfortable. Have your spirit journal and pen with you, and follow me.

Journey on the Path to Material Wealth

You breathe in and out, four times—in through your nose and out through your mouth. Continue breathing, in and out, soft relaxing breaths. Feel your connection to your material self, to the physicality that you are. Let your head tilt back and your eyes fall shut, breathing in and out. Everything through your eyelids becomes gold. The light is very, very gold. Open your spirit eyes and all around you is gold—the walls are gold, the floor is gold, everything is gold. There in the middle of the floor is a big pile of gold rocks, all types of gold. Gold coins, all types of money in a gold light. You might see other objects of material gain—houses, cars, all the things that we think we need to be successful materially.

The gold color intensifies. As you stand listening and looking, you begin to see other colors. Pay attention to the colors you see and in what order you see them. A spirit comes from behind the pile of money. The advisor stands with its hand open, and in its hand there is something. It shows it to you. Look very carefully at what the spirit shows you. This is what you will need to obtain your material wealth. It hands it to you. You hold it, listen to it, feel it, and put it in your mind.

Feel yourself coming back, leaving the gold. You sense the light becoming less and less. You say good-bye to the material wealth, the advisor, and all that was there. You return to your body. You take a breath, continue breathing, open your eyes, and record and interpret what you have seen on this spiritual journey to help you with your material wealth.

JOURNEY OF PROSPERING

Sit where you are comfortable, and breathe in and out. Continue breathing in and out, soft and easy, and relax. Let your mind become the voice. Breathe, and relax. Before you, you will see a path that is a silver shimmer. It is on water. It looks like a sidewalk across the water. You begin walking on that sidewalk. You can feel the cool underneath your feet. The water feels familiar, like a soft pathway. You feel yourself walking into the water; the path goes downhill and you go underneath it. Deeper and deeper you go in the water. The water is above you, beside you, and all around you.

You step through the water and come to a doorway deep within the water, under the earth. The water disappears and you are standing at the doorway. You open the door and step into a brilliant silver-gold light. You walk deep within the goldness and there in front of you is a beautiful waterfall. It is made of color —cascading color. Brilliant colors are before you and bubbles of color splash out around you. Little bubbles and huge bubbles. You see an animal motioning for you to go into the waterfall. That animal is your animal of prospering: it is your guide to prosperity. You step within a certain color in the rainbow. You feel that intensity of color rushing over your body. It may be more than one color, it may be many colors. But remember the prosperity color or colors that you are seeing.

You smell a very fresh smell. Remember that smell, for it is the smell of prosperity. It is the smell that calms your nerves when you need to prosper and when you are prospering. The smell can be anything—flowers, food, weather elements, herbs—but it is your smell of prospering.

The color becomes a path and you follow it into a clearing. There you are joined by your prosperity. Before you, you see yourself doing what you do to prosper. Each time you come here you will be shown the depth of your prospering. You will know by the guidance of the animal of your prosperity, by the color

that you follow, and by the smells that you smell, that you are here within prosperity. Look at what you do, and let it strengthen you, walking you into your fullness of prosperity.

You feel yourself returning to your physicality. You sit quietly in your reality, and listen to the voice of the journey of prosperity. Understand that prospering is not about money, though money is involved, for we live a physical life. But remember that prosperity is the depth of the self, the richness of the spirit, and the knowing. Happiness and security, depth and understanding are yours within the journey of prosperity. Take out your journal, and write down what you have seen, heard, and felt. Know that you have a totem of prosperity, colors, and smells. Find those things and keep them close to you, for they are yours to help you prosper.

JOURNEY OF THE SPIRIT OF MANIFESTATION

Put yourself in a comfortable position and breathe. Breathe one short breath in, and one short, quick breath out. Short breath in, quick breath out. Long, deep breath in, long, deep breath out. Breathe in through your nose and out through your mouth four times, and continue breathing. Before you, you'll see the darkness of night. You will be standing on a mesa, a place where it is flat and wide open to the night sky. Raise your hands into the air spiritually and call for the spirit of manifestation. To manifest, just breathe and listen. You'll hear a sound that will be your manifestation. The sound will be very comforting to you. It could be the sound of traffic, the wind, the ocean, or someone's voice who is familiar and loving to you, but whatever it is, it is the sound of manifestation.

Before you, you see a silver trail made from stars. They are five-pointed stars and they lie flat before you, connected; it is a silver star walkway. You will walk on those stars until you come to a golden line. When you step across that golden line you are standing on a soft, white cloud. You sit cross-legged and snuggle into the cloud, and there in front of you is your spirit of manifestation. This spirit presents itself by sitting cross-legged, opening its hands in front of you. It speaks to you with its expressions, with its color, and with its sound. You see that it is beyond human, but its form is so familiar. It holds out its hand: in its left hand it shows you what you are. In its right hand, you see what you need to manifest.

Remember what it shows you for you must understand it, and then you will know your ability to manifest. The sun shines on the cloud, and the spirit of manifestation becomes a beautiful golden spiral. It begins to spiral out above

you and open up. Peace and tranquility, quiet and wholeness are all around you. You feel yourself totally free within manifestation, and you know that you can do it. Remember what you look like in the hand of manifestation, and remember what you need to become to manifest within your physical existence.

You find yourself sitting in your physical body with your eyes open now, awake and fully in memory of what you have felt—the beauty and the power— and you begin to journal what you have seen and heard, and to look for the interpretations of what lies ahead for you to understand and manifest.

JOURNEY ON THE PATH OF GOOD LUCK

Breathe in and out four times, very softly in through your nose and out through your mouth. You continue breathing softly in and out and relax. Before you, you see a path of soft, green grass that has been walked on, leaving a nice clear walkway for you—a path that leads you into a park area. There is a beautiful blue sky, very green grass; the sun shines brightly; it is morning and birds are singing. You see trees around you, pine trees of different kinds and shapes, maple and oak trees, aspen, willow, cottonwood, evergreen, and cedar trees. There are no people. You walk around in the park looking at the trees and listening to the noise. You come to a little pond, a tiny pond, and there are frogs around it, singing. You feel a twinkling all around you. The color becomes a silver-gold. It seems as if it is misting glitter—golds and silvers.

The sky is very blue. Tiny spirits are dancing along the edges of the pond. One of them points to the pond, and one beside you says, "Look in, and you can see your good luck." You look in the pond and there you can see what your good luck is. It comes to you as a picture, an image that is very clear. It can be a loved one; it can be a place. It will be anything as you look at it, for it is your good luck. They all sing a song of happiness and laughter, for you have seen your good luck in the pond.

Remember what you have seen, taking it in your mind, listening to the happy sounds of the spirits that dance around the pond. You begin to leave, knowing you have your good luck, knowing that you will find a symbol or an object— something that you will keep with you all the time to remind you of your good luck. Come back inside your ordinary physical existence, and breathe in and out. Return to reality where you list in your journal what you have seen, and begin to interpret what good luck is to you.

CHAPTER SIX

*D*EATH *J*OURNEYS

*T*here are often times in our physical existence when we lose people physically, when they die. Death is a teacher, death is a judge, death is an angel. Death is often seen as mercy. Death is unfair, death is fair. Death is a two-sided sword, stronger than the balancing scales that the lady of justice holds, for death is not blind—it has purpose. To understand death and to draw from the power of death is to understand the lessons of life. Death is the greatest lesson of all for it holds within it the power to unbalance, to frighten— as well as holding within it the opportunities, the adventures, and the avenues of difference, change, emptiness, and sadness.

Spiritually, death has no limits, for spirit may always be seen. It may be understood and spoken to, the same as it was when it was in physical form. But you have to believe that. The greatest thing that I can leave with you about death is to remember the Balance that comes from spirits that speak the Truth and give us opportunity. Teachers have lain before us a pathway of adventures that are Truth, that are rich and full. Examples are Nostradamus and Jesus Christ, as well as examples of records in sports, and other records that are broken by someone else's greatness. Examples of Grandness and Greatness are the remnants of physical existence. They are the mind of death, they are our opportunity to remain connected to the ones that we care about.

As you step into the ceremonies of the journeys that lie ahead of you, you need to understand that it is by belief alone that you speak to a spirit who has crossed over. Remember, you are the one who wants to connect with the spirit. The spirit is at peace. It is not a good thing to disturb resting spirits, for they can become angry and make things worse than they were when they were living. It is good to get to a point where you let go and let them be. But, it is important to give a spirit its final rest and you may do so by following the ceremonies of journey that follow.

These are ceremonies that take you to see someone who has crossed over, or that look within your past life connections for the lessons used to mature into your physicality. You can also deal with them by stopping the feelings that would make you want to leave this earth before your time by committing suicide; you can receive a message from the deceased spirit that is important for your protection. This lies ahead of you now in the journeys of death.

JOURNEY TO SEE ONES WHO HAVE CROSSED OVER

Place yourself in a comfortable position and make sure that you are warm. It is important in this ceremony to be as warm as you can be, almost to the point of hot. If you can do this ceremony in a sauna or a hot, hot room, it is safer for you, for you will not feel the coldness that goes along with death.

Breathe in and out, steady long breaths in and out. Remember your breathing and stay connected to your breathing. As you are breathing, you can hear the sound of your heart beating—lub-dub, lub-dub, lub-dub, lub-dub. As you breathe, remember that you want to see one who has crossed over. It is important to keep in mind, as you breathe, why you want to see this loved one. If your intention is to know that he/she is at peace, then state that very clearly within your mind. Continue breathing in and out. Remember that you are never to go to see loved ones to bring harm to yourself or to them. You go there to listen with an open mind and an open heart.

You breathe in and out and before you, you smell chalk, a substance that is choking but mild enough for you to continue to breathe. You remember that you are alive and that you are going to see a living spirit that once lived before. You step through the smoke, and you are standing in a gray haze. You keep walking. You can see nothing ahead of you, just swirls of silent smoke. You step through it and you are standing in the sunshine on a grassy meadow with small flowers around. You can see things—colors and animals, trees and flowers, a river—much like a park. There is a place to sit. There are many places to sit, and you look around and there are people sitting, people walking, coming to and fro from the mist, in and out.

You look around for the ones that you seek. You see them waving at you to come join them. You come and embrace them. You feel their spirit and remember the kindness and goodness that you had, and that you now have in the spirit world. They ask you to sit. You sit with them and ask questions. You ask what you want to know, and they tell you what they want you to hear. You feel the presence of the one that you may no longer see in physical form, and you keep it close to your heart and in your mind. They explain to you what death is, that it is a freedom, that it is life. They show you their true spiritual life. They become free from the form that you knew them to be, and show you themselves as colors, as bursts of energy. Everything becomes a colored gas around you. Your surroundings are no longer what you have known them to be, and everything is rich and full.

You feel warmth and you become aware of yourself in your physical body. You know that the loved one you have come to see is safe. This waits for you just beyond your physical bone. You are no longer sad or disconnected from this person, for you remember their color and you hold it in your heart. Then get your journal and begin to write about what you have seen and heard, and make sense of the messages you received from the one that crossed over.

To understand the journey of past lives is to understand that you have always existed. My belief, my teachings, are that we have always been energy and that before we were physical we were allowed to live with any form for as long as we wished, to learn lessons to prepare for our physical entrance as two-leggeds. I believe, as we cycle through existence, our human life allows us to learn lessons. And lessons are ways to achievement. The success of life is achieved through stamina. Life is a test our spirit experiences to enable the fullness of our spiritual energy.

Journey to Remember Past Lives

Put yourself in a comfortable position and relax by breathing and dismissing stress from your body. Do that by starting at the bottoms of your feet and working up to the top of your head. Feel every part of your body getting heavy and let go of it, until finally you are totally in your head. Then feel your head let go, and you are pure thought. Stand at a door, any door that comes to mind, and open it. When you step in, you will be in the life in which there is a lesson you need to remember. Look around at that place. You could be in a room or you could be outdoors; you could be anywhere—in an airplane, a car, in a battle, any place that comes into your mind. Once you have connected to that life, follow it to its end, and see yourself die with that spirit.

Ask yourself what you have learned from being with that physical existence,

and you will hear the lessons. For example, "I learned how to suffer, I learned how to love. I learned how to be at peace. I learned how to remain intense. I learned how to be gentle."

You may go to this door and go to this place and learn lessons any time you wish. Remember that the end of life is where the lessons are. In life itself you may find it hard to remember every minute or all the things that went on, because it is not your life and you were not there. You come into the life of an existence in which you once belonged and once you go to the end of it, you are in death and can learn your lessons—lessons of power, lessons of discontinuance, lessons of forgiveness—all lessons.

Come back to your physical body. Feel your self reentering. Bring your head back, bring your thoughts out, and work your body all the way down. You become solid and move your fingers, hands, and feet, and you are back in your physical self, where you will record in your journal the lessons you need to learn. That knowledge is given to you as a reminder that you know these lessons, that you have strength and compassion, forgiveness and intensity, that you have impeccability and grandness to carry you through whatever you need in the physical test known as life.

To work with the journey to stop the attraction to suicide, I must note here that suicide is a facet and feeling connected with the illness of depression, that it is a severe mental anxiety. I suggest that if anyone is considering suicide not a moment should pass before consulting a medical official. It would be best to see a psychiatrist, because they are MDs licensed in neurology, and it is a neurological event that is taking place. To speak on suicide is a spiritual matter. Spirit intervenes and proceeds, and also defers. The true chemical neurological problem is in the neurotransmitters within the brain. The question of why people have depression and why they commit suicide is one spiritualists and medical doctors work with every day.

Spiritually, the journey that follows has been given to me to help in the prevention of suicide, but once again I caution, warn and recommend consultation with a psychiatrist when any suicidal feelings come up. It is easy to use the journey and to find peace, but it is also an easy process to gain help through psychiatric intervention.

Journey to Stop the Attraction to Suicide

Sit in a comfortable place and relax. Breathe in and out four times, in through your nose and out through your mouth, and let go of anything that is stressful. Breathe in and out, and clear your mind totally. Do not think of anything. If you feel your mind drifting, take a deep breath in through your nose, and out through your mouth. Focus on the deep, deep, deep color green. Think of only green, and breathe in and out. Check your mind and make sure you are thinking only of green.

Before you, you will see green grass, and the wind will be blowing softly. It is very comfortable to you. The temperature is perfect. The sky is a soft, pale blue, and you see a bunch of green balloons floating up. Follow those balloons. Feel yourself letting go and rising, floating like a balloon—drifting and letting go.

You float downwards, and feel yourself land. You are on a raft and around you, you see soft water. You are very comfortable on the soft, safe raft, floating on a green river in the bright noonday sun. You are just floating, gently floating down the river—not a care in the world. Just relaxed. You feel your raft gently come ashore on the sand. Small pebbles. You look around and there is green grass and a large rock. Sitting on that rock, in the sun, is a turtle. It is green and fairly large. As you look at the turtle, it crawls down off the side of the rock and starts moving away in the grass. You relax. You feel like you want to sleep, and you fall into a deep, deep state of rest. There in your mind, you let go. Feel the sunshine. Open your eyes and there are tree limbs with soft shimmering leaves blowing in the sunlight. You feel at peace with yourself. No thoughts. Nothing but green. Stay there in that thought and breathe in and out.

You feel yourself become solid. You take a deep breath and you are back in your reality. You open your eyes and you have no worries or fears. Just feelings that you wish to write. Maybe something as simple as "My journey was absolutely peaceful." Journal your feelings. Appreciate your life, and understand that things are slow and easy. If you lose that feeling, come back to this journey and go again among the green.

Journey to Learn from Deceased Spirits

Put yourself in a comfortable position, in the brightness of the day, preferably around noontime, or prior to noon. Find a quiet place where you will not be disturbed and sit quietly. Breathe and relax, and continue breathing. Let your mind

focus on where your lessons are to come from. Are you learning a lesson today? Do you need to have answers from someone you have known who is no longer with us—who has died and moved on? Sit quietly and understand that the deceased is at rest. But if there is a need for you to communicate, then let your mind relax and know that you have not let go of the person you wish to communicate with. Understand that the person is there for you to talk with, but that it is important that the lessons you wish to learn from the deceased can be dealt with in your own physicality.

Continue breathing, understanding that the message that you will receive from the spirit is a clean message, that the human you once knew has died and crossed into the spirit world. Think of the spirit world, think of where this person would like to be, the type of atmosphere that the human connects with. Let your mind become quiet and still. Around you is a deep, rich, dark shade of purple. Everything is quiet, and before you, you see a wooden table. With your spirit eyes look at the wooden table. On it is a beautiful white candle, sitting in a very plain candleholder. This candle is burning. Around the flame of the candle you can see an aura of color, many colors. The flame is very still and does not move.

Think of the situation that you have come to learn about. Think of what it is that you want to know. Put that in your mind, focus clearly and watch the candle. Your spirit teacher will join you. When you see the flame on the candle swaying and flickering, you will know that your deceased, in its spirit's form, has joined you. Everything is light and peaceful. You are able to see the spirit of the one who is deceased. It may show itself in its animal form. It may show itself in a color. It may show itself as you remember when it was human. Ask the questions that you want answered. Settle the matters you grieve over. Listen to what this spirit has to say. Look at the gifts that it has brought you. Look at what it is showing you. Remember everything that you see—for everything is a message.

A quietness comes when you are finished, and a wind swishes through and blows out the candle. You are solid in yourself, opening your eyes where you sit, and you know that you have lessons, that you can identify them in words like "discipline" and "obedience," "surrender" and "flow." You remember what your deceased spirit said to you, what you saw, and you journal it. Later you will begin to interpret the lesson that you have learned. Sit with the warmth and understanding of this spirit that you have encountered and learned from.

CHAPTER SEVEN

Marriage Journeys

When going about building a relationship, it is important to remember that it starts with a meeting. One spirit meets another and recognizes it as a familiar spirit—one it feels it has known forever—or it may feel love at first sight. Through the Journey to Find Your Soul Mate and the Journey of the Spirit of Relationship, you are given the opportunity to find the spirit that you are looking for, to understand the depth of what you want to make a commitment to. Life is fast and relationships come and go. It takes dedication and commitment, it takes understanding and perseverance, it takes forgiveness to make cohabitation happen. When marriage comes about, it is a word that brings about reproduction. That is a remolding and a remodeling, a bringing forth a whole new life, a chance of opportunity. In marriage journeys, it is important to look at your own soul. When there are angers and confusions, when there is disconnection and discontent, it is very hard to stay connected to a love that will endure for a lifetime, physically.

So, as you work with your journeys, it is important that you remember that you are a physical being and you have needs. Do you know how to commit? Do you know how to be? Do you know how to find peace within your total self? Is your soul healthy and clean? Good deeds, happy thoughts, and knowing bring this about. Your connection with your family is often the threshold of the future for your new family. For if you have turmoil with father and mother, grandmother and grandfather, aunt and uncle, it is very hard to go into a relationship and make a new, beautiful experience happen. So as you journey and you understand your soul mate, your marriage partner, look at the commitment of love and responsibility that lies within the spirit of relationship. Ask yourself if you are at peace.

Journey to Find Your Soul Mate

Find a quiet, comfortable place where you can relax and be at peace with yourself. Understand your own presence. Think of your strengths, and of your weaknesses. Think of your wants and needs, and your expectations. Get these things really clear in your own mind, and breathe in and out, in and out. Breathe in and out quickly, in and out, in and out. Relax and continue breathing. Before you, you will see bright sunshine. You will see a clearing that is inviting, a place where you can walk. It can be a park, it can be the woods, it can be the ocean. It can be by the lake, or by the river. You begin to walk out there. You see the grass swaying, and you can feel the breeze blowing through your hair. You lift your hands into the spirit, and you breathe, and you think of your needs for companionship. You give a prayer of thankfulness that you have a yearning to have a friend, to have a mate.

Before you, you see a soft blanket lying on the ground. You go there and lie down. The day becomes night and the stars glisten all around you. You feel the softness of the night. You stand; there is a full moon, and everything around you is pale, pale silver. Standing there in front of you is a familiar person, a spirit that reaches its hand out for you. When you look at this spirit, you see color. You see what you would want as a soul mate, as a mate, as someone who you want to spend eternity with. You look at the spirit first, and see the colors. Then, you look at the person and see the size and the hair, the eyes, a distinguishing mark or feature that you would remember. You hold this person in your mind, knowing what he/she would be like if you met in physical existence. Pay very close attention to any smells, any animals, or any colors that you might see, and very close attention to the way the person looks.

Hold this spirit in your mind. Look into the stars and see the glimmering lights. Then feel yourself return to your physical existence, and journal everything that you can to understand and find your soul mate.

Journey of Your Marriage

Find a comfortable place where you won't be disturbed. Sit or lie down and relax. Let all the stress leave your body. Breathe in through your nose deeply, and out through your mouth fully—breathe in and out, and continue breathing. Before you, you see a circle on the ground. This circle is made of rose quartz. It

is laid in the ground like tile—pink and rich and beautiful. It is flat and easy to stand on. The circle is very large. You step up on the circle, and you are standing over the circle of marriage, within friendship and relationship, within partnership and union. You listen, and you hear the sounds of your marriage, places that are important to you as a couple, sounds that you will share for your lifetime. Remember those sounds for they are important to you.

Take a deep breath in and out. Appearing in the circle are the physical things that you will obtain in your marriage. You see your home, your children, the people that are friends within your marriage, your half-side, your partner.

Your spirit feather starts to float from the sky. This is a feather that you use as a prayer feather to hold your marriage together. It floats and falls at your feet. You look at the feather and see what kind it is, what color it is. All around you are flowers, the flowers of your marriage, flowers that hold your union in their smell and their touch. They are your flowers, of your marriage. Remember these flowers.

In the East part of the circle is your totem that protects the spirit of your marriage. You see that animal, or that winged one. In the South you have another. In the West you have another. In the North you have another. Remember these totems for they hold your marriage together.

Stand in the coolness of the pink quartz and remember all the things that you've seen. There is a time that comes to your mind, it is a day of the week—that is a special day for your marriage, for it is the day that you married and you hold that in your mind.

You bring back all these things that you have learned. Solid in your mind, you become physical. Remember what you have seen on the journey of your marriage, journal it, and begin to interpret it, and look at what is so for you and your marriage.

JOURNEY OF THE COMMITMENT OF LOVE

Sit where you will be undisturbed and quiet, comfortable, and safe. Breathe in and out, in through your nose and out through your mouth. Take smooth breaths in and out, in and out, seven times, and continue breathing. Before you, in your mind, you see a white gate. This gate will be beautiful. You will see flowers that coat the gate and make an archway for you to enter. Remember these flowers for they are the flowers of your love.

Before you, you see white stones. Start to walk on these stones. Pay very close attention to what kind of stone they are—what they feel like, what they look like—for they are the strength of the commitment of your love. You walk forward, and you come to an end of the stones. Before you, you will see the commitment of your love. It will take on the form of something in nature—it could be a tree, it could be an ocean, it could be a waterfall. But it will be the commitment of your love. Look at the symbol that is given to you, and remember. Hold it in your mind and bring it back.

Your come back into your physicality and your body is warm and safe. Remember the symbol of the commitment of your love. Journal it, writing everything you know about the symbol that you have seen, for it holds within it the story of the commitment of your love.

JOURNEY OF THE SPIRIT OF RELATIONSHIP

Find a place where you will not be disturbed, and sit or lie down. Breathe in and out. Breathe in very deep and hold your breath. Hold it as long as you can. When you can't hold your breath any longer, let it out, breathe in again, and continue breathing. Before you, you will see color. This color will be very strong. There will be only one color. It will be rich and deep, bright and full. Look at that color, for it is the spirit of relationship within your life. Step within that color. This is the foundation for everything that your relationship is in life, each relationship you have. Become that color. Breathe that color deep inside yourself. Hold the color inside your breath, and know that when you hold a relationship with someone, this is your foundation.

Come back to your physicality, full and rich and deep with the color that is Relationship. Journal the color. Then look in the interpretations guide so that you can begin to understand the color. Understand your principles of Relationship from what you read about the color. Look up the words in the dictionary or thesaurus. Get to know the opposites of the color. Get to know the synonyms of the color. Hold these teachings as guidance within the relationships in your life.

CHAPTER EIGHT

How to Understand and Follow Spiritual Journeys

All of life is thought. Everything in life is a thought. We as human beings are a thought, as is each thing we do and each thought we have. Our thinking enables us to endure. It opens a place for us to step into. When we step into that place, we are in spiritual journey. Understanding spiritual journeys as thoughts allows us to see our physicality as spiritual.

Sometimes in life we follow. We mimic what we have seen before us, for we are very narrow, and not aware of our spiritual thought—the voice, the pathway, the opportunity of knowing, the clairvoyance and psychic ability of a human. When we are in physical form we are separated, for we could be a thought that someone else is thinking. We could be in form because someone thought of us and needed us to be a child, and brought us into human existence.

Understanding spiritual journey as our physical existence is very important on the road of life. When you go into spiritual journey, you deepen your existence. You allow yourself to be in touch with everything that you have to use in order to obtain structure and purpose. Our emotions are voices that guide us. They are pathways that allow us to expand our feelings in negative and positive ways. We are intricately designed as pulsating, electric energy. Our neurosystem is made up of impulses and those impulses are electrical stimuli that cause us to have reality through thought. When we take time to clear our mind and connect with our spiritual journeys, we are given voices that clean, balance, and connect us to our answers. Each of us must remember that as we are in human form, we are pure energy, an image of Great Spirit, Grandfather/Grandmother, Creator. Our opportunities in life are not to be painful, struggling, disconnected, and decayed. They are to unite with the Great Spirit, to be at one with our God, Creator, and open up our existence to the Holy Circle, the Sacred Circle of Life, within the spiral of harmonics. We do that through our spiritual journeys. We give ourselves opportunity through understanding the depth of teachings within color. We do that when we understand the protection that Great Spirit has given us to endure the battles that lie within the thoughts of each opportunity.

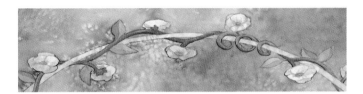

*L*ife is ours to understand and achieve. It is a story that we embark upon and we hold that story as a pathway, as a spiritual journey, in our heart, deep within our mind and the beat of our soul. When we take a spiritual journey to the depth of our soul and listen to the heartbeat of everything, we are dancing life. Each time we spiral through the harmonic existence known as physical form, we cleanse by understanding. Those are our days, when we look at reality and see it as opportunity and choice. We cleanse our pathways. Therefore, our strength is spiritual.

Take time each day to sit and be quiet, to clear your mind. It is good to listen to classical music, or music that has no words. Let the pathways be cleansed by the power of color, smells, and sounds. It is good to bring this to a journal and interpret it, for that shows us our way. Often in life we become connected to what we think is important—money, homes, people, jobs. But what is important is the flow—that the flow is clear and clean. Breathing and connecting with the heartbeat of Great Spirit, Grandmother/ Grandfather take you on a spiritual journey in a warm and safe way, by placing thoughts in your mind through a dream or vision. It allows you to have your Confidence, to see your Truth, to be in your power, and to follow the Will of Great Spirit, Grandmother/Grandfather.

With spiritual journeys you find out who, where, when, and what is important to you. You know where you belong, where there is a deep, solid feeling in your stomach. This solid feeling comes from your mind understanding. In spiritual journeys you have paths, you have color, you have guardians, you have teachers, and you have lessons. In this physical life, it is ours to understand what thought we are. Sometimes we are the marriage of our parents, or we are continued relationships from great-great ancestors into now. We are loyalty, we are structure, we are the next generation. For you as an individual, when you understand that you are thought, and thought is spirit, and you follow your spiritual journey, then you connect with the voices that are necessary for you to find where to go next. Sometimes life is hard, because we feel that we are not in control of our own existence. Sometimes we feel that we have made grave mistakes, and we shouldn't have endured or taken on a certain project. But in your spiritual journeys, if you pay close attention to the sounds and the smells, the animals, the flowers, and the trees, the teachings of each one will bring to you an understanding.

When we apply spiritual journeys to our lives, then we understand that we are in control of our own existence. A habit is ours to set forth; it is ours to break. When we sleep, we allow our thoughts to become pure. In other words, we allow our mind to relax and be cleansed, filing the thoughts that are needed in order to become who we are in physical existence. A lot of the time science is a guess. Often people have been programmed; they don't really have a true knowledge base at all, but are simply carrying on someone else's journey. But when you understand and follow spiritual journeys, you become very clear about your own existence. Wouldn't it be nice to know who you really are and what your spirit really is? Well, then move into the season of your spirit and journey deep inside of yourself. Connect yourself and bring that forth as a belief. You do that by understanding that you are a sacred circle in life—that you are connected to all things and that you cease to be at the moment your thought reaches a higher octave.

Harmonics holds within it higher octaves. Color holds within it more intensity and higher octaves. The brighter the white, the higher the octave. So when we step through and follow our spiritual journey and bring it back to reality, we gather knowledge by understanding what we have learned from our journey through the symbols we have seen.

We connect to the voice of spirit by understanding the meaning of our dreams and visions. We hold the journey sacred in our hearts and love the beauty and strength we have been given.

In religion, we are often looking for our spiritual voice. It is in the sacredness of your journey that you will find your spiritual voice, as you allow yourself to have each thing you do in life be as pure and whole as it can be. If things are well and not contaminated—in other words, if they are not nightmares or bad dreams—then they will carry forth a high octave. If they are nightmares or bad dreams, their octave is low. The high octave is high energy or interest, a desire to bring about new ways in your life.

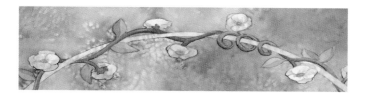

The more you journal about yourself and about your journeying into the spirit realm, the more you will know how to reach a higher octave. The more you follow your own mind, the voice of your soul, the more you will be in tune with Great Spirit. You can see this in the beauty of a waterfall. The highest octaves are represented in the spilling forth of the great force of water. You can also see it in the clear blue sky, and the highest octaves are beyond blue, where the sky turns white. Often the only thing you have to understand your spiritual journey is faith. Let me say one thing: Faith is not abuse. It is not allowing yourself to doubt or fall short of what is true for you. But it is knowing your walk, the sacred medicine that you hold dear, as instructions in your heart. You do not get that from someone else. You find it from the teachings of the earth's purity—the pure water, the pure air, the pure wind, the sitting quiet in the silence of a forest and listening to your deep longings.

When we pursue monetary gain or personal status, we are often filled with greed, anger, and selfishness. When we follow and understand a spiritual journey, we may be asked to let go of things that we call our best friends or money, to let go of places that we feel are home, to let go of people that we know as family. It was said once by a great teacher that we must let go of everything and follow. When we let go and follow our inner voice, we open up to the will of Great Spirit. So to understand and follow a spiritual journey is letting go, finding the purest form we can—exercise, music, laughter, the softness and teachings of nature. Journaling these and making sense of them is our purpose. To teach and bring forth, and give to others mercy, humor, joy, and fulfillment, are our purpose.

It is a good thing every day to journal spiritual journeys that you have had, to learn to separate your dreams and ambitions from a spiritual journey. Write down things you've seen that don't make sense to you, and journal about them until they are plain. If you see a lot of water, for example, maybe it's time to take a trip connected to water.

Study the thoughts that come in a spiritual journey. Only you can make sense of the voice that speaks to you from spiritual realms. Only you can lay a path beyond destruction. Your life is your journey. Your spiritual voice speaks in pictures, colors, sounds, and smells. Take the experiences and bring forth your fullness of life.

Why have you the relationships you do? What journeys do you take? What do you hear when you sleep? It is yours to know the spirit. It is yours to listen to the dead, for they teach you about yourself—beyond the lessons that each of us endure, such as denial, detachment, death. It is yours to decide what you hold as your loyalties.

*L*et me remind you not to cling and hold on to the past, for the word "journey" means to travel forth, to let go of yesterday and walk in today. Holding on to yesterday is simply a crutch. Dear memories are guides, but holding on to them is stifling. To understand your spiritual journeys, you are given a gift of Great Spirit, you are given a gift of the moment of knowledge. Reaching beyond is yours to do through journaling and understanding. Making complete sense out of what you know is spiritual is all that you have to do to feel joy.

CHAPTER NINE

Spiritual Path Journeys

When you are working with spiritual paths, it is important to know that you have a sacred center, that you can communicate from your sacred center through prayer, to your sacred center through prayer, and that you can be guided from your sacred center through your prayer. This allows you to live your life in the fullness of the creation of Great Spirit. When you are walking in your daily life, things are stressful. Moments are stressful. Every emotion affects you. When you balance your life, you obtain your balance by going to your sacred center. It is a place that is very comfortable and familiar. Your mind will project a picture of it, however, and from your sacred center you'll find the peace of mind and tranquility to become quiet. This restores and gives you solid energy, which brings about the color of your life. The color of your life is actions, and actions are sometimes lessons. When you go to your sacred center, it is a familiar place and it is achieved through spiritual path journeys.

JOURNEY TO THE SACRED CENTER

Find a place where you can sit or lie down, where you will feel safe and warm, cool and comfortable. Breathe in through your nose and out through your mouth, in through your nose and out through your mouth. Relax. Continue breathing in and out. Before you, you will see a soft, pale blue. You will feel yourself getting up in your spirit. Standing, you look down and see that you are standing on a dirt path. You begin to walk on that path. You can see nothing around you but blue. You continue walking and breathing in and out. You feel the path going up, and you rise higher in the sky, following the path. You keep walking and the blue becomes a soft mist. It is fog, and it is lifting. You have come to a place that is very familiar to you. It is your sacred center. There is a

place to sit down. There is a place to lie down. There is a ground and a sky.

You look around at your sacred center and become very familiar with this place, for it is a place where you go to find tranquility. You look to your right, and there is a place to sit and you remember what this is. You look to your left and there is a place to lie down, and you remember what this is. You pay close attention to what is around you, what the sky looks like. Is there a ceiling? What the ground looks like. Is there a floor? Are you inside or outside? Are you open to the elements, or closed in? Your sacred center has smells and they are very familiar to you. Is there wildlife there? Is there wilderness? Is there water? What is in your sacred center? What sounds do you hear? What colors do you see? What are the tones like? Are they deep and rich, or high and intense? Are they vast and wide, or narrow and shallow? Pay attention to your sacred center.

Continue breathing. Feel yourself becoming solid. Bring your sacred center from way out there, here, to your physicality, and put it deep inside yourself, in the heart chakra area—in your heart, in your lungs. In your breath is your sacred center. Open your eyes, get your journal, and register what you have seen.

JOURNEY OF PRAYER

Find a place that is very sacred and sit very quietly. Breathe softly in through your nose and out through your mouth, and continue breathing. Breathe very softly and gently. Everything around you will be bright and cheerful. The sun will be shining, birds will be singing. You will be sitting, and in your hands you will hold seven colored beads, and they will form a circle—red, orange, yellow, green, blue, purple, and burgundy. Run the beads through your hands and you will feel the colors.

Speak to Great Spirit and tell the spirit your heart's desire. Pray to Great Spirit—"Oh Great Spirit, hear me. I come to you today listening to the colors that you are, listening to colors that are life. I have many thoughts to share with you. I want to hear you. Speak to me of your wisdom."

Holding your purple bead, pray to listen, to hear the guidance of Great Spirit. There, at your time of prayer, you are answered. You can hear sounds, you can smell smells, you can see colors, wildlife, animal life. You can have a grand conversation with Great Spirit.

All around you are your answers. You listen. You feel. You know. Great Spirit is answering you. "Grandfather/Grandmother, Great Spirit, heal me by showing me and teaching me. Direct me. Give me the strength and the confidence." Your answers come to you and they are very strong. Give thanks for what is shown to you. Open your eyes and see the colors in your hands. Become physical, remembering your prayers and remembering the answers you have heard. Bring them back to your journal, record them, and begin to interpret them. Look for answers, question a life you might have, journal the answer and give thanks to God/Creator/Great Spirit.

JOURNEY OF THE CREATOR OF SPIRIT

Sit very comfortably and relax. You are warm and safe, and you think about your existence—about the planet that you live on, the people around you, the millions and billions of years that creation on planet Earth has existed. You look before you and see solid white sand—glistening sand—full of tiny pieces of crystal. Sparks of color shimmer, flicker and glisten everywhere. You see circles drawn in the sand. You are standing before a powerful oracle, a place known as Center, a place known as Creator of Spirit. There are seven circles—one very large, one inside of that, smaller—down to a point in the Center. There is a line drawn down through the Center and a line drawn across that. The lines meet at a point in the Center.

Step into the Center. There you stand in all of creation. You feel the compassion of mankind; you feel intelligence and well-being. There is no anger, no strife, no hate, no past or present, no future—there is only point, only now. Look up and there is a cylinder of light. You let go in that cylinder of light and become one with the brightest, whitest light that you have ever seen. Your mind no longer thinks: it only feels the intensity of the light. Feel the light rushing through you. Feel yourself one with all present forms of light. Feel yourself falling to the circles, and being distributed as fine points of light in the circles of creation. You feel a spiraling, circling motion intensifying each point of color that brings about your existence. Your mind is clear, your voice is clear, your heart is clear. Your solar plexus is clear, your stomach is clear, your reproductive area is clear. All is clear and you spin into form.

Coming into form, you are standing in your wholeness. You know within your mind all is possible, and that you have answers, for the Creator of Spirit

has given you the opportunity to touch, to feel, to smell, to see, and to hear. Step out of the circle into your solid self. Record what you have felt, what you have heard, what you have seen, for they are mysteries that the Creator of Spirit has shared with you—creating feelings that take you on your own voyage of life. You bring those back to the journal and interpret them.

You will find messages each time you step into the Creator of Spirit Sacred Circle—ways for you to atone and obtain, cleanse and strengthen, and bring forth the miracle of life.

JOURNEY OF THE GREAT SPIRIT PATH

Find a place that is comfortable, sit quietly and clear your mind of everything—think about nothing. Take a deep breath in through your mouth, and out through your mouth. Breathe in slowly through your mouth, and out slowly through your mouth. Continue breathing in through your mouth and out through your mouth—four times. Then breathe in through your nose and out through your mouth, and let your mind become quiet.

Before you, you'll see a path that is inviting. It seems like a path you would want to walk on. You are barefoot and you feel the path. It is sand. You look down, and it is white sand. You walk, and at each side of the path tall grass waves in the wind. The sky is very blue, with soft, wispy, puffy white clouds. You continue walking and you smell familiar aromas. You smell the popcorn from the movies, the ocean air; sounds and smells from a fair become very clear. You smell a pine forest on a rich, cold, winter day. You smell the pine resin on a hot summer day. You smell the city, with all its different odors and sounds. You continue walking this path.

You look out in front of you, and everything has become colors—bright and soft. You see the path weaving its way through the color in front of you. You start to walk in the color, and a problem that you are facing comes to your mind, something you worry about, and the color overcomes the problem. Remember the color that cleanses the problem from your mind. Then you may choose to think about another problem. You know, as you walk along the Path of Great Spirit, that within the colors are ways to go to overcome your problems. As you walk, you are greeted by spirits of wispy color that float like clouds before you—thin, wonderful spirits that sway and dance. Each one of these colored spirits touches you, and your problems are erased and replaced with a color that treats those problems.

Now, as you walk, the path takes you along the ocean. It is mystical here where you stand. A soft breeze blows the ocean air through your hair. You stand and listen, and feel the warmth of the sun and the kindness of the ocean caressing your soul. You look beyond the ocean, and there are colors—wispy spirits swaying, reminding you that each problem you have has been cleansed by Great Spirit's Path.

Remember these colors, and come back to yourself. Feel your physicality, sitting solid in your chair. Reenter, open your eyes, and journal the colors with each problem that you faced. Writing your problems in your journal, put down the colors that you have seen, interpret them and understand that your problems are simply your own choice. There are always answers in the colors, in Great Spirit's Path.

CHAPTER TEN

Taking Something Away and Putting Something Back

Shamanic journeying is a wonderful tool for aligning your energies, affecting your beta and delta rates, influencing your negative and positive ions, and strengthening the energy base known as your kundalini or your sacred chakras, which in turn affect your whole neurological system. Shamanism allows you to step into a world of spirit and hear, feel, and experience the teaching of Great Spirit through vision, symbols, and color, sounds and smells. When you are working with bad habits, sleep-related disorders, empowerment of the self, relationships, learning how to raise children, learning lessons within life, or dealing with understanding the process of death—it is important to remember that whenever you take something away, you put something back.

The philosophy my mother passed on to me, as a teacher of spirituality and visionary guide, is that when we understand our depth of energy, the energy brings itself into physical form through the neurosystem of the body. We are all pure spirit, which is energy, and our own neurosystem is pure energy. Psychiatry has advanced from ordinary shamanism to enriched and updated, vibrant neuropsychiatry. Often we think of spirituality as religion, and don't really understand that shamanism, spirituality, and psychiatry are all the same: that our body is a frequency of color, that our chemistry is electromagnetic energy, that our biorhythms, our delta rates, our REM (Rapid Eye Movement) sleep—all of these are spiritual; that they are governed by our mind, and that our mind touches the component system known as our brain and allows us to physically exist.

I think later on in time, when scientists realize that we are a hologram of spirit, then we can go to the base, which is Great Spirit, and adjust the picture. But it seems to take a long time for people to come to the realization that

when they take something away, they have to replace it. For when you weaken physically, you should intensify spiritually. When you bring that intensification to physicality, it should be guarded, it should be taken care of. What would hurt it? Words. Words are beings—tempting, alluring, dangerous, competitive, envious, greedy, defying, ignorant, bad, evil. All of these words subject us to a weakening of our spiritual system, which weakens our neurological system. Extreme bursts of trauma—yelling, fighting, arguing, fear—bring about post-traumatic stress. Battle, defending our rights, pushing our energy base far beyond its normal ability, brings about post-traumatic stress. This is a true disorder in the psychiatric field, which destroys hundreds of thousands of people every year. The stress of driving a car or living in a bad relationship, keeping on, thinking that it will change someday, can totally annihilate the spiritual structure known as your kundalini.

Your kundalini is the protective energy that surges power into your chakras, energy channels that feed and bring forth the physical existence of your neurons. When you reach out in spirit, in shamanic journey such as the one in this book, you take something away that you don't like and you put something back that you do like. Remember that you have spiritual guards. These are protectors. They are spirits of color that take on form—the form of animals or a spirit form. They can take the form of a guardian angel, diva, nature spirit, or an object of the four elements that protect you and your home. They come to bring balance and spirit to your life.

It is important to remember that you want wholeness, that you want spirituality to be in its totality in your life. Sometimes for us to get the most out of our life we have to seek out therapy. There is nothing to be ashamed about in needing some physical interaction.

Sometimes our chemistry is bad, and it is important to see a psychiatrist. I refer to psychiatry, because shamanism is the begining of psychiatry and chemistry. The physical existence that psychiatrists work with is the end of the path known as human existence. We have come a long way from energy to energy, working with spirits and understanding energy. Working with chemicals and understanding spirit is a total circle of life. Moving through rainbow journeys you allow yourself to have the very best. So we have gone from an old way—vision and shamanism—to a new way, neuropsychiatry. I do recommend counseling. I recommend teachings. I recommend religious beliefs. I recommend faith more than anything. But it is important to remember that sometimes your body malfunctions and it is important to take it in and have it aligned and tuned the very best that you can.

Be present in those meetings. Do research. Apply yourself to the fullest, and your life will be beyond your expectations. For when you take the "bad" out of your life and you put the "good" into it, the good Red Road leads you into the sunrise of tomorrow. You can rely upon colors, the interpretations, and frequencies that lie within stones, the teachings and the medicines within herbs and trees. You can depend on the smells, the chemicals, the effervescence of life itself—physical and spiritual. You can put your faith in your guides and your guards. You can put your faith in your spiritual ancestors, teachers of great lessons, and you can have a rich, full sacred circle known as the human existence.

But it is very important to remember that when you take something away, you put something back. When you let go of a bad thought or experience, replace it with a good one.

CHAPTER ELEVEN

Removing Bad Habit Journeys

Journey to Overcome Alcohol and Drug Abuse

Find a place where you can sit or lie down, a quiet, warm place where you won't be disturbed. Before you start your journey, think about what it is that you wish to remove. Is it alcohol? Is it a drug? It is important to focus on what it is, the alcohol or drug. Take a few minutes to see yourself with your vice, to see yourself with your best friend that you call alcohol or drug. Think about how much money it costs, and what you have to do to get that money—how you take that money away from something else in your life. Think about how the drug or the alcohol comes into your life and what it does—how it makes you work harder, or lie, or steal—how it takes away physical wealth and monetary gain that you could apply in other places in your life. Be realistic about what you are thinking. How many dollars do you spend? How many hours does it take? What do you drink, and when do you drink it? What drug do you take, and when do you take it? Ask yourself, "Do you know what alcohol is for? what its purpose is?" Ask yourself, "Do you know the drug you take? what herb it is? what chemical formula it is? what it is made for, why it exists in the first place?"

Now think of the word "pleasure." Think of the pleasure you get from taking the alcohol or the drug. Is it true pleasure? Pleasure is without guilt. It is without harm to others. It is without lies. It doesn't hold grudges. It doesn't hold, control, or dictate. Pleasure is free; it is flow. It is a certain part of the brain that reacts healthfully. When you enter into a relationship with alcohol or drugs, your brain is craving; it is crying out to balance its neurochemistry.

Look before you, and let your mind relax. Close your eyes, and breathe in and out. Before you, you'll see a fresh water creek with water rushing down. The air is clean and clear. Walk to the creek, and in your mind's eye take out the drug you use. Taste the drug; then taste the clear water. Clarity has no substance to

poison you. It has no temporary fix for chemicals that have gone astray in your mind. The substance that you are using is a poison, a temporary adjustment for a neurochemical situation. Your mind is craving something that alcohol or drugs cannot give it.

Kneel by the water and wash your face in the creek. Rise up, take the substance that you use, and pour it into the air. It will change into yellowish, green lights that fall like water drops and land on the water. The water neutralizes their color and they become silver. The substance that you craved floats away, and so does your craving for false treatment. You drink from the water, and there before you, you see a beautiful path—a walk in the woods with flowers, eucalyptus, Boston ferns, and pines. Animals are grazing and playing in the trees and on the ground. You see all the things that life has to offer—butterflies, and children playing. Peace comes to your soul and you drink more of the water. Words like friendship, strength, and obedience come to your mind.

Look down the river where the the substance that you crave floats away, and for you it is fresh water. Stand and remember what you have seen, what animals stand out in your mind—what plants, and what rocks? What sounds do you hear? And most of all, remember the clean, fresh water that you drink.

Come back to your journal. Feel yourself solid in your body and write down what you have seen. Every time you go for a substance that you want to call a party or a good time, remember that you are escaping. Remember that it is not pleasure but poison, and that it separates you from that which makes you whole—the fresh babbling creek of life. As you journey in your mind over and over to fight the addictions, call out for help.

Seek out medical help. Seek out those that you can trust—spiritualists, psychiatrists, counselors, programs that help you. Each day when you drink from the babbling creek, the pure flow of life, you grow stronger in your healing. You find a way to strengthen your life into wholeness.

Journey to Overcome Smoking

Find a place that is quiet and comfortable, where you can sit and not be disturbed. Breathe in and out six times, quickly, in through your nose and out through your mouth. The seventh time, breathe in deeply through your mouth and out through your mouth, easy and slow. Then continue breathing in and out through your nose. Before you, you see a doorway. Go to the door and open it. Step out into a majestic blue. Everything around you is blue, but you can see the landscape, you can see the ground. It is very, very cold. So cold that the cold burns. Make peace with the cold. Be the cold. Feel the cold become warm through the burning.

You feel a calmness come over you. It is quiet. You are very much in control. You hear a voice say, "Would you like a cigarette?" Think of your cigarette, how you reach for it without a direct thought—how you often have no intention of smoking, but you find yourself smoking. The wind blows and you feel the cold. Hold a cigarette in your hands. Look at the cigarette and you see the cigarette turn blue. You feel the cold. You take a deep breath in through your nose, and you blow out smoke over the blue cigarette. You watch the cigarette turn to smoke. You breathe in the cool air, and you blow out smoke.

Every time you choose to smoke, take a deep breath in and blow out smoke. Continue breathing, and be grateful for the fact that you don't smoke. Each time you choose to have a cigarette, remember that they are blue. Breathe in and blow out smoke, and choose not to smoke. See yourself becoming stronger. See your lungs becoming healed.

Feel yourself coming back to your solid self. Feel yourself in your body. With eyes open, journal what you have felt. Each day write in your journal about Truth. Do you believe you should smoke? Do you believe you shouldn't smoke? Journaling about smoking, you realize that you want to quit, and that you have full control over whether or not you take a cigarette. This helps you to quit.

Remember that while you are healing from nicotine you will have cravings that will make you want to eat. Remember the rule: when you take something away, you replace something. When you want to smoke, you don't want to replace it with eating. You want to replace it with exercise. Often exercise feels like a hard thing to do, but replace the urge to smoke with going for an easy walk, or a soft swim, or ride a horse, or go for a drive in your car. Take a shower or a bubble bath, or sit in the hot tub. These are a few things that help you to replace the urge to smoke with something more productive. Journal each day what you replaced the urges with and enjoy a smoke-free life.

Journey to Overcome Eating Disorders

Find a place where you can sit or lie down, where you are comfortable and undisturbed. When you sit or lie down, think about what your favorite foods are, and then think about why you like them. Does it make you happy to eat these foods? Or do you just find yourself eating them because it gives you a good feeling? Or do you realize that you don't even know what your favorite foods are and you eat constantly—it doesn't matter what it is—you just eat? Think about things that you don't like to eat, and why you don't like them. Understand and remember that having a proper eating structure means giving your body what it needs. Understand that you should have a well-rounded diet with choices of different kinds of foods—choices of different breakfast foods, choices of different lunches, choices of different vegetables and fruits.

It is very important, remember, that you eat for your body, not just to eat what you want. When we eat foods we want, we're acting upon choices that have been made out of anger or fear, or as a defense against abandonment or loneliness. It is very important to remember that sugar and fats are very addictive.

Take a deep breath in through your nose, and let it out. Clear your mind, and relax. Continue breathing in and out, and remember this sentence: "When you take something away or change something, you put something back or do something different." It is important to remember, as you are breathing, that what you put back brings about success and happiness, and is different from what you have always done.

Before you, you see a very quiet and calm place. A place where the grass is green and the sky is blue. As you look at this place, you see yourself walk into it, but not the way you are—the way you want to be. Watch yourself sit and rest. You are not afraid. You are not living in the past; you are not living up to someone else's expectations. You are not sad, but you are happy, rested, relaxed. Your weight is exactly what you want it to be. You look good, and you feel good. Watch yourself get up and go for a walk. You are very relaxed, very happy and well-balanced. You are not pushing or stressing yourself.

Watch yourself walk to the edge of a lake where there is a pile of rocks. Listen to yourself: "Each one of these rocks is a bad habit that I have when it comes to eating, and I am letting it go." Watch yourself pick up one rock and say, "This is my bad habit of not taking time for breakfast, lunch, and dinner," and throw it into the water. The next rock you pick up: "This is my bad habit of not liking foods that are good for me," and you throw it in the water. Pick up another rock and hear yourself say, "This is my bad habit of eating too many fats and not paying attention to how much saturated fat and cholesterol I put into my body," and throw it into the water. Pick up another rock: "This is for using alcohol and too much sugar, and eating without paying any attention to the number of objects I have placed in my mouth," and throw it into the water. When you see yourself pick up the last rock: "This is for not exercising, taking walks, playing games, moving around and using energy," and throw it into the water.

Then you see yourself celebrating, clapping, jumping up and down, and being ecstatic about the fact that you no longer have the weight of these rocks in your life. You become yourself now, and there is only one person standing there—you. Take a deep breath in, and as you do, you see all seven colors of the rainbow. The beautiful colors become your mind, and you say to yourself, "I have the confidence to be balanced. To bring about creativity that allows me to grow. From living my truth and understanding my wisdom I obtain my impeccability. I can do this every day and celebrate."

Look out at the water and remember the things that keep you from having your weight under control. Begin to walk back to your physical life, knowing that each time a "bad" thing happens to you in life, you can go to the water and throw it away. See the bad happening being released from your life. Most of all, remember that you are good enough, and that you deserve to have a happy life. Come into your solid self, open your eyes, and journal how you feel. When you are journaling about overeating, look at the things you do that you know you shouldn't do, and write those down. Remember that when you take something away, you put something back. So when you take away a bad habit, put a good one back. When you journal about things that you "shouldn't" be doing, then you must solve the dilemma by putting something down that you "should" be doing.

Through shamanism you can go within the journey and see yourself the way you want to be. You can construct yourself the way you want by giving yourself assignments in the spirit, such as breathing, being happy, seeing yourself strong, and watching yourself do an exercise routine in the spirit before you do it physically. But the important thing about an eating disorder is to remember that it is an emotional disorder, that it comes from an imbalance in your anger, in your fear, in a lack of acceptance and self-esteem, which often is brought about by child abuse. When you have an eating disorder, you might want to seek professional help, for eating disorders may be chemical behavioral problems, and you might need the assistance of a psychiatrist.

It is important to remember that any disorder can be something where you find great joy, for you understand that you are out of control and you begin to question happiness and success. Go for help, set goals, and make life changes. It is your life. Live, be happy, have fun.

When you take spiritual journeys to work with eating disorders, you can bring your spirit totems, your spirit guides and your animal guides to strengthen you on your path when you feel weak. See them in your journey. Think of their life. Learn about them and follow their example. All relations in the spirit want to bring strength, beauty, and goodness to your path.

Journey to Feel Safe and Overcome Bad Luck

Find a place where you can lie down or sit, and not be disturbed. Sit and think for a few moments about your safety, and your luck. Being safe and having good luck are very much the same thing, for safety is Strength. It is solidity, compassion, understanding, Confidence, and Truth, and good luck is the movement of Wisdom, Truth, and Confidence. Good luck is the energy of Creativity expanding in your life. Remember that when you set your intention to be safe, you are working with discipline. You are looking constantly and paying attention; you are aware of what others are thinking and doing. For you to have good luck is to prevent bad luck. Your good luck comes with the intention and intensity of color.

Breathe in deeply through your nose, and out through your mouth—in through your nose, and out through your mouth, and continue breathing, in and out. You are in the sunshine, and it is warm and safe. You are lying on your back, and the ground is very cool and very solid. The sun puts a web over you. This web is made of all different colors. It is warm and strong. The web is energy that radiates far beyond your Earth, way into the center core of the spirit world. From the very essence of Great Spirit this web comes forth, and expands in its silver hues. It glistens with reds and purples and burgundies, with turquoise and greens, oranges and yellows. It surrounds you.

You are lying in this web, breathing in and out. The word "acceptance" comes to mind. To accept things as they are is your safety. You hear a voice state very clearly, "Accepting things as they are is your safety." You are protected by the wonderful hues of color reflecting in the sun from the Great

Spirit's web, and you have only good luck.

Good luck is not money. It is not fame and riches, or who you are with. It is not material things, but it is the adventure. It is the opportunity and the acceptance in your life. You look before you, through the web, and you can see what your good luck consists of.

Words of intention become your wealth. The way you treat others becomes your prosperity. The kindness you bestow upon your family becomes your riches. You see a good home. You see beautiful flowers. You see good weather. You see good luck for yourself.

Lie there inside the web and feel your heart beating. Every time it beats, the color grows stronger in front of you; like waves in a pond, it ripples out. Watch those colors, for you can interpret them and apply them to your life as medicine. They will teach what you need to know in order to have the strongest and best luck possible.

Feel yourself solid, open your eyes, and you are back in your physicality. Note in your journal what colors you need. Look them up and listen to the medicine words and the lesson words you need to apply in your life. Do this, and act upon these words, and you will have good luck, for this journey is a prevention of bad luck.

CHAPTER TWELVE

Sleep-Related Journeys

Sleep is a mystical place. It is a scientific necessity for the physical existence. It is a mystery. Something that alters or changes your sleep can weaken your whole existence. In the following journeys I write about nightmares, sound sleep, stopping sleepless nights, and dreamtime. They are four very interesting topics and very different.

A lot of information is available on sleep, and a lot of studies have been done in the last twenty years. It has been proven and is well known that the brain is like a computer in that it sorts memories and files them by remembering and discharging them. When you have a nightmare, it seems very scary to you, and it may haunt you throughout the day. This is known as sleep haunting.

But it is important to remember that nightmares are giving your brain the chance to heal from the intense stimuli that it has encountered during the day. Most of the time nightmares are extreme fears that are being sorted through and filed so that you can soon get rid of the fears.

It isn't unusual to have a recurring nightmare for a long, long time, but the following journeys help to speed up the process of sorting and settling nightmares. Sound sleep is essential for your brain to relax, and to allow your synapse processes, which are energy charges, to take place properly. When you sleep soundly, you go into what is known as REM sleep. REM sleep is necessary for you to function well the next day. It is important that you get to a deep level of brain waves to achieve your sound sleep.

Sleeplessness can be related to clinical depression, a true illness that needs medical treatment. Sleeplessness, or insomnia, can be symptomatic of several different medical situations. From a spiritual viewpoint, it can often be cured by having a strong connection with a spirit guide and relaxing and knowing that you are safe. But if you are restless and sleepless with what you think of as true insomnia, then you need to seek out a psychiatrist or some other therapist who works in that area.

Dreamtime is a mysterious place to a physician. If you diagnose it as a sickness, you don't truly understand it. Dreamtime is a mystery, a place you can step into and be all-knowing, a place where you can understand your fantasies and live out your physical realities. Often the experiences in dreamtime are known as premonitions.

You are in a state of dreamtime when you project the future in your sleep. During dreamtime, you feel as if you are actually there physically. It is not like a normal dream—it is very lucid, very transparent, and the characters seem so real. This is where you have stepped into dreamtime, and have the opportunity to see the way life will go, before you actually make the choice physically. You are dreaming out your life so that you can understand it and be prepared for it in your reality. Many times we dream out life before we live it. Keep up with your dreams and set goals to achieve a dream life.

Often dreamtime teachers and dreamtime experiences will prepare you for tragic or unwanted events in your future. So I suggest you pay very close attention to your dreamtime and draw lessons from what is brought to you when you are in that state of mind. I am giving you a journey that allows you to step into dreamtime and know that you are there. Then you will be more clear on what you see, know, and need to do with what you have seen.

Journey to Stop Nightmares

Sit on the side of the bed just before you are going to sleep, and take a deep breath in through your nose and out through your mouth. Continue breathing and relax. Breathe in and out, several ordinary breaths, then take in one deep breath through your nose and out through your mouth. Think for a moment. Your brain houses all your thinking power. It is made up of neurological charges. Your brain is similar to a computer; it has to file your fears. Take the next few seconds and breathe in and out very deeply through your nose and out through your mouth, and let your fear come into balance. Clear your mind. Think only peaceful thoughts, good thoughts.

Lie down on the bed, get comfortable, and take a deep breath in through your nose, and let it out. Close your eyes and you will begin to see a color. That color will be very clear to you—very solid and strong, crystal clear, soft, and beautiful. Turn that color into a blanket and spread it over your physical body in your spirit thought. See yourself covered in a blanket of this color. Become very quiet, very still, and very peaceful. Hear the sounds that you like to listen to—children playing, a television set, a radio, wind blowing, ocean, cars in the city, total silence, birds chirping, horses whinnying—whatever sounds bring you great joy and comfort.

In your presence you begin to sense someone, someone very soft and kind, loving and tender. Your sleep guardian is with you now. You can see that spirit, and it will have an animal helper with it to protect you. This will be a familiar animal to you—one that may be your favorite, one that you might own, one that you would feel comfortable with. See your spirit guardian petting the animal. It asks you to go with them. You leave your physical body and move deeper into your spirit. Start to walk, turning and seeing your physical body covered in the blanket. You go with your animal helper and your sleep guardian. They take you to a place that is very comfortable and you all get ready for rest. There are places to sleep, and you and your protector find your places. Your animal sleeps at your feet and you go into a very deep state of rest.

You will awake in the morning feeling very peaceful. Your brain will have filed its fears, and you will remember your new companions. You can meet them any time that you need to. When you awaken, journal what you need to—who your guide is, who your animal protector is, what your place looks like—because you may have different experiences every time.

Journey to Sound Sleep

Sit on the side of your bed, just before you are ready to go to sleep, and remember that your brain is like a computer. The purpose of your brain is to channel all the electrical stimuli that work your nervous system, that keep you alive and full of energy. You say a prayer of thankfulness, that you understand your brain better. Raise your arms in the air, stretch, and take a deep breath in through your mouth and out through your nose—in through your mouth, and out through your nose. Do this four times. The fourth time put your arms down, lie down on your bed, and get very comfortable.

Close your eyes. Everything in front of you is blue—just a beautiful, deep, rich shade of blue. Feel yourself lying on a very soft piece of air, and being the most comfortable you have ever been. Breathe in and out. Concentrate on your soft breathing in and out. Breathe in once, and that breath is red. Relax by breathing out. Breathe in two times in and out. Think of the color orange, breathe that thought, and relax. Breathe in again, and that breath is yellow. Breathe in again, and that breath is green. Breathe in and out, and that breath is blue. Breathe purple in, and out. Breathe burgundy in, and out. Continue breathing, and now feel yourself floating on water. Feel the ripples underneath you—as you float on the water. Feel yourself becoming the water.

Relax and let go. You are the water. Go deeper within the water, and it gets darker blue. Darker and darker and darker. Go into a very deep sleep where you can feel and sense all the shades of blue and all the colors reflecting, floating, singing. You sleep very deeply.

Wake up to your alarm, feeling very rested, very strong, and powerful. The water is within you. Journal your feelings from the night before. Write what your journey of sound sleep felt like to you, things that you might have heard, things you might have seen, and your interpretation of the messages. Look forward to another night's sound sleep.

Note: Not sleeping properly is very serious and needs to be looked at carefully. You may need to consult a physician. You can put the following Horse journey together with any medical treatment.

Journey to Stop Sleepless Nights

Sleepless nights cause irritability and induce great stress in your life. Suffering from sleeplessness allows an angry person to remain angry and increases dysfunction in families, as well as domestic violence. There are four steps to stop sleepless nights:

1. Have a thorough psychiatric evaluation or consult a neurologist to make sure your chemical balance is correct. If you choose not to take care of yourself in a medical way, it is very dangerous. It is true, though, that sleeplessness can be aided through spiritual connections.

2. Keep a sleep journal, writing down the time you go to bed, the time you go to sleep, and the time you wake up. Keep track of things in your sleep journal, such as: being too cold or too warm, needing to have darkness or light, and needing to have noise or silence while you sleep. Journal if you can sleep alone, or if you need someone. Be dedicated to your sleep journal for at least six months, but better still, keep it always, because it allows you to know the depth of yourself.

3. Stopping sleepless nights can be as simple as changing your diet. Beware of late meals, large amounts of food, or an absence of food. A combination of poor diet, too little exercise, or too much exercise can lead to sleepless nights.

4. Follow the journey to stop sleepless nights. Go to the place where you intend to sleep. Lie in a position in which you feel you can fall asleep. Shut your eyes and breathe in and out gently through your nose. Continue breathing softly and relax. Clear your mind and see total darkness in front of you. Begin to see (as if in a dream) a beautiful place that is familiar to you—for example, a shady, lush, green spot where you can lie down. (It can be any season, place, and any time of day.) A horse will come to you. This horse can look any way you want. Allow yourself to touch the horse—play with it, groom it, talk to it, chase it, and follow it. Let the journey expand into its fullness. The sleep horse will carry you away into a soft sleep. This journey ends when you awake up.

JOURNEY OF DREAMTIME

Dreamtime is a place in the spirit world where you go to listen to teachings of your ancestors, of your guardian spirits, of your animal helpers and spirit teachers, ones who show you the way. It is also a place where you can receive warnings and guidance, where you will gain great wisdom that will help you understand your physical world. When you go into dreamtime, you are accessing both teachings of spirit and the deep emotions of your fantasies. So it is in dreamtime that the realities of your physical life and guidance of the spirit world come together.

It is important to journal everything about your dreamtime experiences. They will seem very real, so you need to take time with your journal. The most troubling parts of the dreamtime experience are things that you have to cope with, organize, dismiss, and understand in your physical existence. Pay very close attention to the spiritual guidance you get from your protecting spirits or animal helpers, or the colors that help you heal what you are dealing with in your everyday life.

It is best to go into dreamtime in the early morning or the afternoon. I don't advise it before nighttime sleep. The strongest point of dreamtime is right after you wake up in the morning.

Find a place where you can sit or lie down. Relax by breathing in through your nose and out through your mouth—quick, easy breaths. Breathe this way

for several breaths, quickly, in through your nose and out through your mouth. Then draw a deep, full breath in through your nose and out through your mouth. If this brings about a yawn, it is very good. Breathe in through your nose, and out through your mouth. At this point, allow your eyes to close and your head to fall back deep into your pillow. In front of you, you will see a spiraling white light with yellow around its edges. Concentrate on the center of the white light. This will begin your dreamtime experience. You will see things that may or may not make sense to you. You will be given your dreamtime experience through what feels like a movie, or a broken pattern of thoughts. Let this experience happen on its own, watching and listening, sensing and smelling, hearing and tasting everything you have to achieve from dreamtime.

There will come a time when you feel like leaving dreamtime. You must keep moving unless it is your time to leave. When you can hear two thoughts: (1) Come back, I know I must come back, and (2) I need to leave—one of them coming back and one of them departing, then you can leave dreamtime. You will see yourself exit through the bright, white light again, and return to your physical state where you will journal what you have seen. Don't try to make sense of what you have seen in dreamtime, but write it down.

Example: A propeller of an airplane. A coastline. A duck flying north. Everything turns to white, soft clouds. A wonderful smell of springtime. And the voice calling me back, the voice saying I need to go.

Your dreamtime experience can come in many different ways. Another example: You could have a clear illustrated picture of an accident that is going to occur—a car burning, a house burning, a tornado, a devastating flood, car accidents. You see this, recognize who's in it, and recognize that it is in the future. This is the premonitional quality of dreamtime, warning you that you might want to change what you are doing. You can avoid the situation by not doing what you had planned, or by making changes—not by avoiding what you were going to do, but praying that you can change the energy, and that you don't need the accident to teach you lessons.

Journal everything about your dreamtime experience. It may not make sense to you at all until you journal it and look it up in the interpretations. Then you will start to understand the situation you are working with.

CHAPTER THIRTEEN

EMPOWERMENT JOURNEYS

I like to look at empowerment as an energy surge, or solid energy. Each person has a level of energy that is his or her empowerment. You need your empowerment to strive and be successful, to achieve, and to maintain. Using the following Rainbow Empowerment Journeys, you may bring about power to balance your chakras, the energy openings in your body. You have one in the top of your head, one in your forehead between your eyes, one in the center of your throat, one in your heart area, one at your solar plexus area, one in your stomach, and one in your reproductive area. These spots are where energy moves in and out of your body. Your chakras are tunnels. When I think of them I picture tubes, like paper towel tubes. They are energy tubes. They are not physical and they run through your body, from front to back and from top to bottom.

The one at the top of your head connects with all your chakras. The energy surges through all your chakras from the top of your head, as well as through the front of your head, the front of your body and out through the back. When your chakras are fully balanced and in order, they are about the size of a quarter. If they were expanded, they could be anywhere from the size of a fifty-cent piece up to the size of a silver dollar. If you are drained and closed down, the chakras could get as small as a dime. You can see your chakras only through creative visualization, through shamanic journeying, through relaxing and looking through your spirit eyes. You cannot feel your chakras physically unless you have been trained to do so. If you feel them you will sense the resonance of the power of your energy reducing or intensifying.

It is important to remember, when you are empowering yourself, that you draw upon the seven colors—red, orange, yellow, green, blue, purple, and burgundy. These colors are words; they are the energies that give you your words. They are the energies that give you your physical existence. The resonation of your chakras all being in balance is known as your kundalini. Your kundalini is

the energy force around you that is often seen as an aura. The following journeys help you strengthen your energy system, and produce a constant flowing energy. As your being intensifies, the energy strengthens. The chakras are a life support system to full spiritual energy.

Empowerment is necessary and you can get it in many ways. Shamanic journeying is one of them. Other things that help you to empower yourself are being organized, being disciplined, having a proper diet and daily exercise, and making sure that your nervous system, the neurological chemistry in your brain, is balanced properly—in other words, that you're not suffering from depression or any chemical imbalances. Empowerment also can come through prayer and meditation, good medical balance, cleansing, balancing, and strengthening your kundalini system, your chakras, The things that help with empowerment are pleasure, happy places, good memories, positive thinking, kindness, warmth, color, and other interactions with energy: such as rocks and elements—rain, sun, snow, wind, fire, earth. Having strong self-empowerment is being a total sacred circle.

JOURNEY OF SELF-EMPOWERMENT

Find a place where you can sit or lie down, where you won't be disturbed. Sit there, lie there, and take a deep breath in through your nose, and out through your mouth. Then breathe in through your mouth and out through your mouth—in through your mouth, and out. In and out. Continue breathing in through your nose and out through your mouth.

Before you, you see a grassy place that is very comfortable. The sky is blue and it is sunny. Walk to that spot and stand there—join the spirit of yourself. Raise your arms into the air, and take a deep breath. As you do, everything turns red. As you breathe out, it softens to pink. Move your arms down a little, and breathe in—everything turns orange. Breathe out, and it is a soft peach color. Move your arms down a little, breathe in, and everything turns yellow. Breathe out and it is a soft, pale yellow. Move your arms down a little more, breathe in and everything turns green. Breathe out, and everything is a soft green. Move your arms down a little and breathe in, and everything turns blue. Breathe out, and everything is a soft blue. Move your arms down a little, breathe in and everything is purple. Breathe out, and it is a soft purple. Move your arms down and let them gently touch your sides. Breathe in and everything is a burgundy. Breathe out, and everything is a soft mauve.

Continue breathing, in and out. Open your spirit eyes, and look. Before you, you see swirling color. This is the color you need more of; this is the color you need to strengthen. Breathe that color in, and it is really deep and rich. Breathe out, and it is soft and easy. Look and see if you still see color. If you do, breathe it in—rich and full, and out—soft and gentle. If you see no color, then you are empowered and you are in balance.

Come back to your physical existence comfortably, warmly, softly. Open your eyes and journal the color that you have just seen. Interpret it, and write in your journal about how you will achieve more of what it stands for in your life. Remembering your self-empowerment journey, know that you are balanced and that your colors are strong. You know what you need, from the interpretation of the color, to be empowered.

Journey to Balance Your Chakras

Find a place where you will be quiet, warm, comfortable, and undisturbed. Sit or lie down. Breathe in through your nose and out through your mouth. Breathe in, and out. Feel yourself becoming very heavy and very solid. Your spirit will step out of your physical existence, and you will see through your spirit's eyes. Look back at your physical body. It is sitting very still, and very quiet, with its eyes closed. Your spirit will look at the reproductive area of your body, and there you will see a glowing light. The light will be red. It will be coming out of a cylindrical, round-shaped hole. Look at the light and see what size it is. Is it as big as a quarter, a fifty-cent piece, a silver dollar, or bigger? Is it as small as a nickel, a penny, a dime, or smaller?

You will want the red light to be the size of a quarter. If it is bigger, you will make it smaller. If it is small, you will make it larger, until the vibrating light is the size of a quarter. With your spiritual hand, point at your chakra, and work the energy. Work it clockwise if the chakra is too small, expanding it to quarter-size. Then hold your hand in a stopped position, and hold the color there, the size of a quarter. If it is too large, run your hand counterclockwise and move the color down to the size of a quarter. Put your hand in a stopped position, and hold the color at that size.

Once your color is the size of a quarter, move your hand in a waving motion from front to back, and move the energy clearly through your chakra tunnel. See the wave of color moving through the channel itself.

When you have finished your red, move to the stomach area and you will see the pulsating color in the stomach area, the orange chakra. Look and see the size of the chakra and adjust it the same way, finishing with the waving motion of your hand, running the energy—vibrating and pulsing—through the cylinder itself.

Move up to the solar plexus area. This area is right at the bottom of the rib cage, in the center—your upper stomach area. Look for the color, which will be yellow, and adjust the size. If your chakras are quarter-size, simply brush the energy with your waving hand motion. If not, adjust the size.

Move up to the green chakra, which is in the heart area. Adjust the size and smooth the color frequency with your spiritual wave.

When you are finished, move to the blue chakra, which is in the throat. Adjust the size and check the frequency, and move on to the purple chakra, which is right between your eyes, in your forehead. Adjust the size of the chakra and move on and look at the top of your head. There you will see the burgundy chakra, which runs down through your body. Adjust this chakra, and the wave of frequency that runs through it.

When you are finished, back up and look at your body, and you will see rays of light in all seven colors moving in and out of your body. It will be beautiful and balanced.

Rejoin your body by walking forward, turning around, and reentering your physical existence. You will take a deep breath, open your eyes, and feel the balance of the colors in your body. The energies that give life to your existence are now balanced. Record in your journal the sizes of your different chakras, and look at your interpretations. If the chakra was so big that you had to push too hard, your energies were expanding in that color. If they were too much, you have had too much stress in your life, or you are not doing what you really want to do, and there is a need for acceptance or change. If they were too small, it means that you had not increased the energy of that color and that you need more of it, more of that action to expand and keep your chakras in the appropriate colors.

The interpretations of the colors will reveal the areas that the chakras influence in your life. If you are having difficulty in a certain area of life, you might want to check that chakra each day and make sure it is balanced and structured in the way that it needs to be. It is important to keep your chakras balanced by river, taking a nice bath and relaxing, and visualizing your chakras in balance. Touch base with your chakras as often as four times a day, to keep everything in balance.

Journey of the Inner Rainbow of Peace

Sit where you are warm, comfortable, quiet, and will not be disturbed. You breathe in through your nose, quickly, and out through mouth. Do this seven times—breathing in and out quickly. After the seventh breath, take a deep, slow breath in and let it out very slowly. Before your eyes, the room becomes very, very dull. Close your eyes and everything is quiet. In front of you, you see silver—a silver floor, very sparkly, very, very strong and powerful. You begin to walk on the silver, and everything is clear.

Follow the silver until it becomes green grass. It will take you down the side of a little sloping hill. The air will be very cool, crisp, and thin. You get to the bottom of the hill and sit. In the sky, there is a wonderful rainbow. It is right in front of you, arcing up into the air. You are at the spot where it comes down and touches the ground. Lie back, raise your arms above your head, and let the rainbow baste you with color. Breathe in the colors—each one a soft mist. The first color is ..., the second color is..., the third color is..., the fourth color is..., the fifth, the sixth, the seventh. As each color comes in, you see a different object. These objects may be anything. Sit up and see that the rainbow is gone. Think of the seven objects that came to you. Each one of them will teach you about its connection to the color it came in with. Remember the object and the color.

Become solid and come back. Open your eyes, and record the colors and the objects. Listen to what they have to say and journal what applies to your life. As you come to understand the interpretations, you become peaceful, for you realize what is necessary for you. Sometimes only one color or one objects speaks to you. Sometimes all the objects and all the colors speak, but you will find your own peace and make your own sense of what you have seen within your Journey of the Inner Rainbow of Peace.

JOURNEY TO RECEIVE HEALING

This journey is to enable you to feel better, to have the breath of empowerment when you are not feeling well. It can work with a simple sadness or a severe illness. It helps you to be at peace and to have acceptance.

Sit where you are quiet and not disturbed, and have fresh air blowing on you. Take a deep breath and feel the fresh air as you let your breath out. Take another, and let the ill feelings go into the fresh air. Before you, you will see a stairway. Start to climb those stairs. As you do, you will feel weak, but as you climb them you will feel stronger and stronger. Breathe in and out as you take each step. When you reach the top of the stairs, there will be a path that will lead you into clouds. Follow that path and walk into the clouds. Continue walking. You will come to a gate that is wide open, and you will step into the place that you see. Look at what you see. Listen to what you see. Do not try to force it or make it happen—just see what you see.

Remember what you have seen, and bring it back, holding it in your mind. Let go, and you will float within your self. You will regain your solidity, and you will breathe in through your mouth and out through your nose. When you open your eyes, you will feel strong and rested, empowered in what you have seen. Record it in your journal, and think about how wonderful what it has to say to you is. Take this message and listen very carefully, and you will feel better. You will be in acceptance.

CHAPTER FOURTEEN

CHILDREN JOURNEYS

Children journeys allow you to walk within what you know as a child. These journeys are designed for you to be able to communicate, see, construct, understand, raise, and create what we call children. The four journeys that I will take you on now will allow you to open up, step past your fantasy, and go to a more practical reality of what your children are, what they can be, what you have to offer them from your DNA connection—what we call physical, which is nothing more than a resonance of color brought forth as actions.

Find a place where you are warm and safe, cool and comfortable. Have your journal and a pen with you, and follow me now.

JOURNEY TO SEE THE SPIRIT OF YOUR CHILDREN

Breathe in and out. Do this four times, and relax. You will feel soft and restful. Let yourself just drift into thought, freeing yourself from your mind. Before you, see a yard with green grass, a park with green grass—a place that is cheerful and playful. Notice what is there. Notice that there are toys and fun things. Look around and see what fun you can find. Watch and see the power and the color within play. In this space now, you start to hear laughter. Little teeny, tiny laughs. Lots of children's joy ringing out around you. Laughter of teenagers, laughter of young people. Voices of soft little girls.

Look now, and you will see children. All around you. All ages, all sizes, all shapes, all colors. Look beyond what you remember as their human form and see them for what they truly are. You may see only color. You may see flowers. You may see leaves on trees. Animals—you may only see their color. You may only hear their sound. Pay very close attention, for there will be the ones that are yours. Look and you will see them as sparks, brighter than others. Listen,

and you will hear them, louder than others. Look there, and capture that thought, for you see your children at that moment—you see your child.

Look at what it looks like, and what it sounds like. Listen. Breathe in and out. Relax and understand. It is a precious moment for you to hold the spirit side of your child. It is your future, the resonance of your ongoing existence. Thank it. Tell it "Thank you" for being there. Let go.

You will feel yourself coming back, walking through the place of the children, coming back into the room where you are. You will feel and know that you are in your body. Open your eyes and write in your journal what you have seen. You have journeyed to see the spirit of your children.

Journey to Understand How to Raise Your Children

Breathe in four times, in and out. Relax and allow yourself to be at peace, thinking no thoughts. Before you is a path, and you will walk on it. You will feel the earth beneath your feet. You will see before you a large walk, and beside it a smaller rock—a place where you can sit. You sit down on the stone and you can feel it underneath your hands. You look down at the ground between your feet, and there is a crystal clear water puddle. It is soft and fluid and you can look into it. There you see your children. You see them at all various ages, and you see yourself interacting with them. You see yourself talking to your children, and them talking to you. Listen, and you can hear the conversation.

You look ahead and you see their future, as you know it to be. You turn to your children and ask them, would they like what you saw. Let them answer you, and listen to what they say. You ask them, "What would you like in your future?" You watch their faces and pay attention to what they look like. They want to be in the now. They run. You watch them go into the now, being and doing what they are.

Look over the things they have to choose from. You see the physical things such as food and clothing, going to school. Look beyond that. You will see what they need in the wind speaking to them. You will see the colors extending from their hands and softly touching them, the colors are angels, touching their faces. You will see the joy in their play, in their learning. Look at the spirit of each of these things. It could be color. It could be a knowing. Allow it to be the guidance that speaks to you in raising your children.

Let go of these thoughts now, and you are looking at the puddle. You can feel the rock. You get up and walk back into yourself.

You reattach to the physical moment you live in. You breathe carefully, open your eyes and journal what you have felt for your children. Let it go forward and allow you to raise your children. Go to this place often and gather knowledge to raise your children.

JOURNEY OF CREATIVITY TO ENRICH YOUR CHILD'S SPIRIT

Breathe in and out four times. Continue breathing softly, and relax. You will feel yourself rising, going upward, leaving your home, leaving the place where you are now—going outside, leaving the earth. Look before you and you will see a path. Look at the substance of this path, for it is important to know the path that you walk on: it is the path that is Creativity. Look at it carefully, for you need it for the creativity of your children. Let this path take you to their creative needs. Look in front of you and you will see the spirit of your children's creativity. It can be a simple setting, a place where they play, rest, learn, a place where they are of spirit. Look at this place. Listen to it. Breathe in and out and hold this place in your spirit.

Look around. Who is there? How do they communicate? What do you hear? There can be silence and softness. There can be rest. There can be fullness, excitement, hustle and bustle. You know—you are there now. This place that you see—hold it in thought now—is the creativity of your children. The very spiritual core of their needs.

An example to help you here: soft breezes, pastel clouds, smells of spring rain, fresh wood. Abstract color, tinkling bells, a dog barking. As you write this example, think what it can be in the reality of your children right now. Maybe they need a dog to play with. Maybe they need to go to the park and learn about clouds, and look beyond them to the spirit that lies there waiting on them. Maybe they are resting, and you need just to look at them and appreciate the beauty of the different colors of their faces.

You feel yourself settling, falling back into yourself. You come back in softly and comfortably, taking a deep breath and remembering the creativity of your children, your child.

This journey allows you to soften and to hold in your mind your love for your children, a strong spiritual connection. Breathe deeply and return to yourself. Open your eyes and look around. Journal what you have seen.

JOURNEY TO SEE THE JOY OF YOUR CHILDREN

Breathe in and out four times. Continue breathing softly and relax. You feel yourself letting go of everything around you. Feel yourself separating the spirit from the physical. Your spirit looks forward and there in front of you is green grass. Rising from the green grass are tiny lights. These lights come up one at a time. Look and see a number of lights—count them. The lights are all different colors. The first one is long, the second one is longer. Count them and look at their colors. The lights rise and go higher into the sky, and you watch them disappear. Remember how many lights you have seen and what each of their colors is.

You feel yourself breathing and your spirit moving back within the warmth of your physicality. You feel yourself solid, a human being, a physical person, and you know that you have seen the joy of your children. You come back to your journal and record what you have seen, knowing that in the interpretation of this vision, you know what brings joy to your children.

In a spiritual journey there are no teachings. This is the fun part of this chapter. You interpret what you have seen. You get to make it the way you want it to be. I will give you an example here to help you bring about your wholeness through spiritual journeying. Each thing you have felt and each thing you have heard is a reflection of spirit as you would like it to be, or as it is, and you can't change that. Often beings just are what they are at the moment, but, remember that spirit is constantly moving. It is constant in itself and moving in energy.

Let your thoughts interpret your journey. For example, the spirit of my child looked like a yellow daffodil. It was jumping and playing and running and it lay down and took a nap. I interpret it to mean my child is quick and in need of nurturing in the field of art and drama and I should allow my child to dance, take it to the park where it can blow soap bubbles and play; let it lie on the grass and rest; build it a soft little pallet on the floor and let it nurture itself in rest. My child is a joyful, cheerful, resting person.

It is easy to interpret your spiritual journeying. Just allow your mind to flow and write down what you want it to be. Then those thoughts propel themselves outward and manifest themselves as actions, and you'll find it won't be long until you will truly be living the spirit, the understanding and the creativity of your children. And they will have a full spiritual existence where you will allow them to be.

CHAPTER FIFTEEN

*I*NTERPRETATIONS, *M*EDICINE, *S*HAMANIC *U*NDERSTANDING

*W*hen you take shamanic journeys, each type of shamanism reflects on the interpretations. I am using general Native American interpretations, which come from all different types of thoughts and feelings throughout the total Native American population of America. It is important to remember, when you go to interpret a shamanic journey, that often things are simply symbolic. Journeying differs very much from dreams, and dreamtime, as I have mentioned previously, differs very much from dreams.

The interpretations in Rainbow Spirit Journeys are given to you as medicine. Some categories within life are true medicine. Within shamanism there are no omens, no superstitions, no predictions—there is only applied truth, applied understanding. There are no warnings. There is information and a message. So when you take a shamanic journey and see, for example, a television set, an automobile, a young girl crying—these are things that your mind is cleaning up, filing, and sorting. They are not the messages themselves. The messages are in the interpretation categories that follow.

Medicines are voices. Medicine is often looked at as a cure, something that you buy in a bottle and take to get well—such as pills that make you feel better, chemical connections that align your body, surgery that alters, and things that rearrange your life. The medicine I wish to teach is applied faith, applied truth—it is growth, understanding, learning, discipline, communication, commitment, responsibility, and relationship—it is the companionship that brings about the advice to guide you.

When you interpret a rainbow journey, look at the interpretation category and understand that only a few areas in life are true message bearers. Medicine is a voice, or voices, from the spirit world that bring about a clear understanding of your direction. So when you are interpreting a rainbow journey and you see an automobile, a girl crying, or a television set, it is important that you write that down in your journal and understand what you are dealing with in your everyday existence. Our mind, our brain, is capable of so much. It has often been said that in life humans only use three percent of their brain. That systematic, physical object files and computes, but it is our consciousness in which we understand what we're seeing and make sense out of that which makes us who we are.

Within a shamanic journey you see and transmit energy. That energy is the voice of your spirit. When you go within your shamanic journeys, go past the dream state where the filing and the sorting takes place, where the messages, the superstitions, and the clarifications, take place. Move on into a state of communication that is known as "walking in two worlds," which is what shamanism is. The understanding of messages from the spirit worlds and the message bearers themselves—spirits that carry teachings, objects that bring vibrational frequency to your life—set you in motion to be what you are. For example: In our homes we have plants; we put rocks in our homes; we have certain colors; we have animals. Those are not just objects. They are medicines. They are things that bring us great joy. The plants bring oxygen to our lives; the animals bring about companionship and friendship. They also tell us when something is approaching, something that our ears might not be capable of hearing, be it in the physical world or the spiritual world.

I am giving you information in the interpretations in this book that will help you to begin to understand what you need to hear from the spirit world. You are always welcome to go on and express your own feelings, and to bring about your own interpretations from your own journeys. That is what spiritual journeys are about—for you to establish a personal relationship with the spirit world. In shamanism there are no intermediates; there is no one who is better than you, who can interpret better than you, for it is your own spiritual journey that you are embarking upon.

The only warning that I would place here in the interpretations is to make sure that the definitions and the interpretations you find come from your own needs and wants—not from someone else's teachings, doctrine, or religious standpoint or even from a spiritual happening.

It is important to understand the difference between a need and a want to interpret a rainbow journey. A want is something that you learn a lesson from, something that takes you through life and opens up doorways for you to gain greater knowledge, greater wisdom, greater power. Example: You want a diamond ring. It takes money to buy the ring, and to obtain money you must work, and to work you must get along with other people. Sometimes you have to do things that you don't want to do because they are too physically strenuous. Sometimes you do things that are very hard because your mind is not capable of bringing forth the type of thinking needed. So to obtain a simple diamond ring is a very long process of working, earning, saving, and purchasing. Once you have the ring you have to take care of it, protect it, clean it, put it in the proper place, and then you have to figure out what to do with it when you are done with it. So a want is something that brings about a circle of great adventure and sometimes intense situations.

A need is a part of your personality. It is a piece of your very essence. You need color, air, energy, companionship, shelter, food, and good health. These things are seen and answered by the fact that if you did not have them, you would not exist. If you didn't have air, you wouldn't be able to breathe, and, therefore, you wouldn't live. If you didn't have companionship, you would become lonely, despondent, and eventually die. If you didn't have shelter you could freeze to death. The wisdom, the power, the truth, and the logic of life lie within what you need. Things that are very profound, such as joy and happiness, are brought about by the connection to another. That can be a spirit, a human being, a four-legged, a winged one, a crawly, that brings great joy to your life and allows you to go on.

So when you interpret your shamanic journeys, it is a simple process. Is there something you need or something you want? That will help you with the monetary objects that come up in your visions, because frequently they are going to be a need or a want. They are often an emotion—something you are angry at, happy about, sad from, afraid of, disgusted with, or something that you need to accept. So when you are interpreting inanimate or plain objects or other things in your shamanic journey, ask yourself if it is emotional and then put it into one or more of the seven basic emotions. Is it something that you accept, that you are disgusted with, that brings you happiness, sadness, anger, fear, or joy? Then you will be able to determine the medicines that have messages and show you the path—not predictions, not superstitions, but things that give you a good, clear path. We call that the Red Road—something spiritual that you can walk on in your physicality. You will be able to tell them quickly from inanimate objects, objects of emotion, things that bring about a want in your life.

When you journey and you journal, it is important to understand what your wants and needs are. Keep yourself centered, which means remaining focused on what you are doing, and calm—not childish, hyper, aggressive, and anxious about what you are looking for. I like to think of life as an easy path that wanders along, not a mysterious, hidden, unattainable trip.

Rainbow journey interpretation example: automobile, crying girl, and television set. The automobile is a symbol of movement; the crying girl is the symbol of releasing; and the TV is a symbol of creativity. The way I come up with the interpretation of the objects is to ask myself, What does the object mean to me? I list out the facts about the object (there might be many), and then I narrow them down to the ones that mean the most to me. Feel free to brainstorm different topics within a vision and you will come up with the answer to your interpretation of your journey. The journey I have given you says to me that it is time to move on, release everything around you, and be creative. Trust your mind to interpret the voice of your shamanic journey and be guaranteed that you will have a spiritual adventure.

I wish you good luck, lots of fun and joy in your interpretations using rainbow journeys.

MEDICINE INTERPRETATIONS

NUMBERS

1—The number one represents wholeness and strength, the ability to bring about things yourself, to reach within the circle of sacred knowledge which is your mother, father, grandmother, grandfather, great-grandmother, great-grandfather, aunts, and uncles. Look within your own family structure to bring about the strongest traits and live them as yourself. One is red and also pink.

2—Two speaks about ability. It is a gathering number, one that brings about choices and courage. It is a number that resonates, bringing about equality and taking care of situations. It is orange and pale orange.

3—Number three is a triangle, a number of making your point clear. It has the energy of bringing forth, creating and resonating happiness. It is a storyteller and a poet. It is yellow, and pale yellow.

4—Number four is the number of movement and action. It teaches; it has tricks and treats within it. It is the number of spiritual doorways, the entrance from which the spirits come and go; ancestors and teachers of knowledge communicate using this number. It is the personality of beauty and the depth of sadness. It is green and pale green.

5—Number five is the number of solidity, the number of truth. It is a doorway that brings about your deepest longings and desires. It reflects your personality. It is the number of tranquility; it is blue and pale blue.

6—Number six is a pathway, a support system, a number that holds great wisdom and power. The number of commitment, of the regal and the royal, it is evidence and longevity. It is purple and lavender.

7—Number seven is intensity—teaching, inspiring, divining and manifesting. It is a number of intrigue and mystery, of enhancement and richness, of fullness, and spirituality. It is burgundy and pale mauve.

8—A number that stands on its own, it is the number of the center. It is the resonation of self, the combustion of color, the spiral staircase of enhancement and life. It also is the number of death. It is white, and therefore it resonates with all the colors.

9—Number nine is complete—the number of materialization and matter. It is the number of human nature. It is wholeness and totality, existence. It is black.

SHAPES

Circle—It is the shape of the sacred, the symbol of life. Its number is eight, its color is white.

Rectangle—It is a doorway. It is opportunity, and longevity, thinking and seeking. It is number nine, and it is black.

Triangle—It is the symbol of power, wisdom, knowledge, and attainment. It is number six. It is purple.

Square—It is the foundation, points of respect. It is the avenues in which spirits come together. It is number four, and it is green.

Octagon—It is mystery, development, expansion, learning, and teaching. It is the number seven. It is the color burgundy.

Line—It is absolute, straight, and complete. It is a pathway, an opportunity. It is number one. It is red.

Curve—It is energy. It is spiraling. It is challenging. It is unseen. It is happy. It is the number three. It is yellow.

COLORS

Red—is Confidence, the ability that you can do anything you choose to do. It is Strength, an action that is motivated by ability and knowledge, belief and faith. It is Nurture and Colors. Red is influenced by all that is. To have the ability, to be Accountable, which is what red is, is to draw from all colors and to bring forth. It is Accountability, the ability of all colors, the spokesman, the strength and velocity of energy.

Orange—is Balance, being able to understand that you are physical, that there are things that happen that are outside of your power, things that go beyond yourself that are the choices of other people. It is success, organizing, having discipline, being committed and dedicated to bring forth an issue, to make an action happen. It is Choice, looking, reasoning, asking yourself what your Choice entails, and what will be ahead of you. It is the pure existence of everything. It brings forth, it enables. It is responsibility, taking on a project and understanding the beginning, the middle, and the end.

Yellow—is Creativity, the ability to bring forth, to design, to cultivate, to make something happen by sitting and planning. It is art and music, happiness, drama, humor. It is vision, the ability to look beyond and make sense of a thought, a picture that guides you and brings about goals. It is ceremony, the procedure that brings things to fruition. It is prayer, the communication with spirit and physical that brings about messages and clarity, that builds understanding, and makes your tasks come to be. It is sincerity, an absence of lies, an absence of vanity, of emotions, and anger. It is the completion and whole honesty.

Green—is Growth, the perpetual motion which life is. It is your opportunity to see your existence, purpose. It is beauty, the pretty, the sparkle, the enhancement that beauty is. It is change, the ability to know things are not as you want them to be and move to bring about your desires in a fair and loving way. It is honest, truthful, dependable, comprehensible. Green is playful and young. It holds within it the story of sadness. It has the ability to teach quiet, patient ways. It is quiet, restful, still.

Blue—is Truth, what is so. It is healing, for it brings knowledge, facts, and outcomes. Truth is doing good, feeling good, and bringing forth honor and success. It is agreed on by all as right.

It brings about comfort. It is safe and warm, cool and comfortable. It is proof, facts and stories, solid beliefs brought forth that you can depend on. It is tranquility, an absence of expectation. It just is. It is faithfulness, for it is always there. It is what you count on, like your breath and your heartbeat.

Purple—is Wisdom, many hours of gathering your Knowledge and studying, bringing forth a reality that you will teach and spread to others. It is power, knowing that what you have is stronger than money or physicality, for it is made of respect. It is real, it has been and always will be. It can be tried in the test of time, and it will always be physically what it is. It is the legacy of your cellular abilities, things that come from generation to generation and are passed on. It is the way that you achieve. It is commitment, applying yourself, dedicating yourself, knowing the structure you need to achieve your dreams and goals.

Burgundy—is Impeccability, the absolute in life that is the correct way. It is what is great, the feelings that you work hard to achieve, the perfection of everything. It is grandness, a gift that is bestowed upon you by others, when you meet the goal of what they expect, when you hold the answers and those answers are present. It is the will. Burgundy is the flow of existence that comes about whether we want to admit it or not. It is the outcome and the point; it is purpose. It is mystery. It makes it possible to know the unknown through the usage of all the colors. Burgundy is the answer to the unknown. When the unknown comes forward, it will be with great intensity, great learning, and great dedication. Grandness itself is obtained by the will of Great Spirit. It comes when you give your best and bring honor to what you are doing.

White—is the element of all, everything. It is the bright energy that gives us the ability to know. It is ability, spirituality, spirit.

Black—is totality, obtaining and having physicality, things that you wish for, things that you want. It is wholeness, your needs met, the ability to bring about what you want for your fullness.

Silver—is spiritual movement and color. It is energy that brings about the spiritual. It is the shimmer, the sparkle, and the glisten, the twinkle and resonance of joy.

Gold—is obtaining matter. It is success through your wants. It is the ability to have. It conjures, it attracts, it brings about solidity.

Turquoise—is the color of spiritual protection surrounding you. It strengthens you and allows your safety to resonate through everything you choose to have in life. It is a spiritual recognition of respectful religion. It is brightness and newness. It is the color of tomorrow—it always predicts there is something to live for beyond today. It is sacred and holy.

TREES

Trees hold within them the grandness and greatness of stability. They speak of an inner core of strength. Trees have the ability to work as recorders and hold within ancient wisdom that brings about peace.

Alder—The resonance of knowing oneself. Orange energy, balance of the self, being able to look within and draw the knowledge of "good" and understand and reject "bad." Alders help us find integrity, bring about peace of mind, and give us harmony within our spirit.

Apple—Speaks of romance. Apple trees give us the time to renew our romance, to have within our grasp and live the act of love. They are the love medicine tree. They hold within their spirit the secrets of sexual desire and passion.

Ash—Gives us understanding and compassion, sincerity and truth. It is the doorway. The action of sincerity comes from holding the spirit of ash in your soul.

Aspen—The one that catches your eye. Aspens are the ones who know. They are your intuition and help you within intuition. They give you the ability to discern, and they assist you with ceremonies of forgiveness.

Birch—Holds within it green teachings. Birches are quiet, tolerant, and they help you to have psychic ability, to look and to listen, to think, and bring about realization.

Cedar—A ceremonial tree. It is used in cleansing ceremonies to release and purify your spirit. It helps with renewal and replacement. It is a strong friend in time of need, in time of grief.

Cherry—Speaks to our drive, helps us to produce and bring about success. It is often known as an achievement tree, for it bears strong fruit, has the ability to produce, and teaches us to be inspired to physical productivity.

Dogwood—The tree of spiritual inspiration. It is a storyteller and has the ability to bring about harmony and to distinguish between the unknown and the known.

Eucalyptus—A clearing, cleansing tree. It brings about transformation, transmutation, nurturing, and kindness.

Fir—An elder of ancient wisdom. It can be used for purification, restoration, and regeneration of knowledge. You can sit in the quietness of its presence and learn.

Fire Maple—Assists you with intense energy. Come fall, you'll see it in the red-orange of the fire maple. It uplifts your integrity and strengthens you when depression is about. It lifts from a lull to a high pitch.

Fruit Trees—The medicine of bringing forth, creating. A fruit tree embodies the story of the medicine wheel, teaching the full circle from beginning to end. It shows abundance and prosperity. Each fruit describes the needs that you might study.

Hemlock—A poison tree that signals warning and care. It is about banishing and doing away with, cleansing.

Maple—The weather tree. It is the tree that tells you that you have strength, the tree of luck and prosperity. It signals a change in the weather and shows us that we can tell when we need water, and when water is coming.

Oak—The tree of steadfastness. It holds within it stability and power, might and perfection. Carrying an acorn with you will bring protection. This protection gives you the ability to center yourself and know not to fear those things that can harm your spirit.

Pear—A tree of hope and faith. It speaks of growth and generosity.

Pine—Holds within it the song of life, tranquility, impeccability, the story of eternal life in all its greenness, the ever-present beauty of ancient wisdom.

Poplar—Vision, taking time for achievement through ceremony and drawing peace within your spirit.

Redwood—Maturity in your emotions, memory, longevity, and strength. The knowledge that when you reach deep inside, you will have what you need in life.

Walnut—Confidence and energy, the tree of solid, hard, obtainable ways.

Willow—Mystic visions. The ability of open clairvoyance, the powers of your third eye, being psychic. To bend with the wind and go with the flow. Continuing, bending, friendship, and luck.

HERBS AND VEGETABLES

Cedar—Used to clear and cleanse your fears and anger, to connect with Great Spirit and listen, bringing about the ceremony of cleansing.

Cornmeal—Used to prepare sacred space, to balance the energy fields, to bring about positivity, to cleanse negative ions, also to feed your spirit guides and communicate with your spirit helpers. To welcome the spirits of the light kind.

Juniper—Used for clearing and cleansing negative energies. The purifier used in protection, to balance fear. Use when you have a need to work with your fears, to move out negative ions and bring about positive ones.

Piñon—Used to cleanse your energy fields, releasing all angers and negative feelings. Use to welcome spirit helpers, to look into the sky and see the spirits speak. Protection.

Sage—A balancer, one that brings about clean air, honor. Fresh, balanced, positive ions. Clarity and freshness.

Sandalwood—Allows you to seek harmony, to open up to a harmonious balance. Used to bring peace to old wounds and angers, open the psychic ability, look for clarity, communicate with your spirit helpers.

Sweet grass—A settling of the mind. A peacefulness within your spirit. Helps work with angry toxins, helps center and clear, energize, and balance your mind.

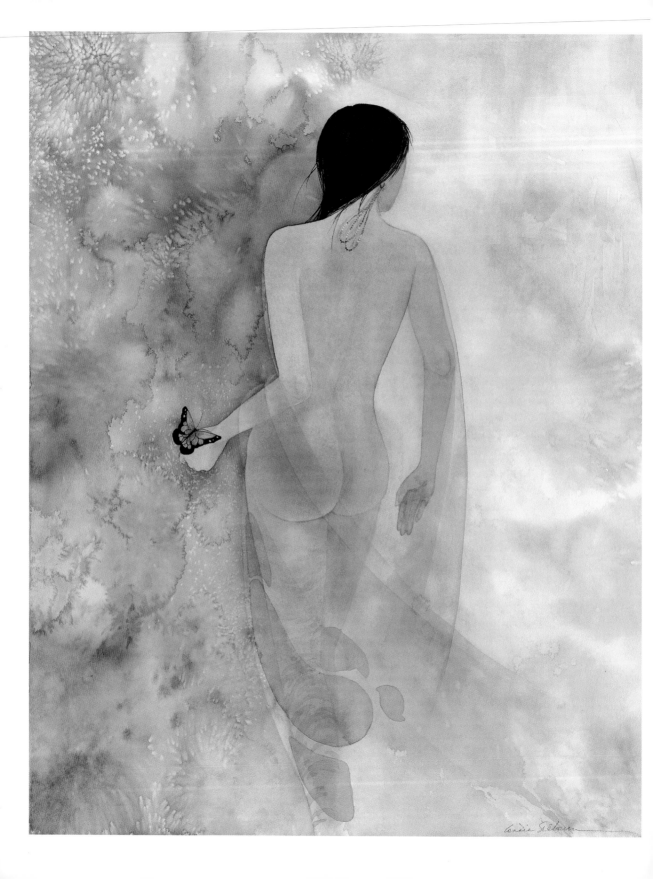

INSECTS—THE CRAWLIES

Ant—Patience, hard work, togetherness, order, rules.

Beetle—Purpose, coming about, movement, naivety.

Butterfly—Beauty, faith, change, sacredness, the circle, opening, the beginning and end, transformation.

Centipede (thousand-legged)—Touching, awareness, sincerity.

Cockroach—Bringing forth, reproducing, forever, eternal, long-lasting.

Dragonfly—Vision, knowing, dreamtime, illusion, a doorway.

Ladybug—Planning, work, money, good fortune, luck.

Lightning bug—Spirituality, magic, creativity, enhancement, play, joy.

Potato bug (or roly-poly)—Childhood, protection, play, safety, kindness.

Scorpion—Survival, intelligence, depth, strength, intensity.

Slug—Unconditional, keeping on, slow, smooth, no limit.

Snail—Comfort, security, warmth, home.

Spider—Trickster, storyteller, learning, teaching, hearing, listening, knowledge.

FOUR-LEGGED—THE ANIMALS

The animals are symbolic of the words that go along with them. Each animal has the symbolic meaning given below, as I know it.

Antelope—Fast, quick, change, movement, action.

Bear—Wise, chief, fierce, introspection, parent.

Beaver—Hard work, perseverance, stubborn, steadfast.

Bobcat—Playful, serious, intense, intelligent.

Buffalo—Provider, totality, prayer.

Cougar—Sly, strong, capable, noble.

Deer—Gentle, fine, quick, motion.

Dog—Loyal, kind, fierce, trainable.

Elk—Romance, leadership, strength.

Fox—Clever, keen, sharp, smart, quick.
Horse—Worker, friend, loyal, wild, freedom.
Lynx—Hidden thoughts, secrets, containment.
Mink—Wealth, prosperity.
Moose—Self-esteem, easy, grand, gentle.
Mouse—Sharp, smart, keen, fun, happy-go-lucky.
Otter—Grace, survivor, woman energy.
Prairie Dog—Family, relationship, helper, protector.
Ram—Noble, quick, intense.
Raccoon—Family, simple, curiosity.
Skunk—Confidence, aware, reputation.
Squirrel—Gatherer, smart, prepared.
Weasel—Crafty, contained, severe, survival.
Wolf—Teacher, leader, path, parent, guide.

THE ROOT PEOPLE—PLANTS AND FLOWERS

Angelica—Points out anxiety. It works with weakness, hopelessness, and helps balance the aura and bring about clarity.

Balm—A need for protection. Lets you know when you are dealing with melancholy, anger, rage, and sadness. It will bring the voice of soothing tranquility to restless sleep or sleeplessness.

Bergamot—This plant tells you that you have a lot of excess stress, and that you need encouragement. It helps to bring about encouraging vibrations. It lets you know that there is nervous tension in your neuro-system. It helps to calm and bring about peace.

Carnation—They come to you to guide you into uplifting feelings. They help in time of grief. They speak of dots of color that bring joy to your life. They are refreshing, pleasant, and nurturing.

Cedar—Speaks to you of fear in the air, that you have anger, and that there is psychological disconnection. It recommends a calming, warming, harmonious and comfortable atmosphere—pointing out that you need to take time and honor yourself.

Chamomile—Shows that there is a need to deal with your tension, that you may be overworked or overly sensitive. It brings about calm and helps you understand and receive messages clearly.

Cypress—Points out that maybe you are forgetful, that there are things that are being overlooked. It works with weak-mindedness and sexual cravings. It seeks a gentle atmosphere and helps you collect your thoughts.

Daisies—Marriage, youth of women, times of celebration and ceremony.

Eucalyptus—This plant says that you are struggling and need to balance, to look at what is stimulating your focus. Take time to sit with your emotional overload. Organize and plan.

Geraniums—Tell that there are days of comfort and harmony, that the sun will come out and it will shine for you tomorrow.

Grapefruit—Speaks of harmony, balance, and confronting issues to help bring about comfort.

Honey clover—Tells that you need to go to a place, and are seeking a place, with a gentle atmosphere and rest. It is a time for calm and sensitivity.

Hyssop—Asks you to examine your extreme mood swings. It asks you to deal with your overworking, pointing out that you must beware of extreme fatigue. It tells you that it is time to refresh and slow down, to cleanse, to use meditation to focus and to become clear.

Irises—Speak of spring, new beginnings, a time to start new projects, the new moon, beauty, and choices.

Jasmine—When you have gone as low as you can go and your self-esteem is at its breaking point, jasmine tells you that there is comfort in its fragrance; it aids the emotions and stops suffering and fear. It brings forth strong confidence.

Juniper—Aids with workaholism. It tells you that there is more to life than pushing yourself beyond your boundaries.

Lavender—A refreshing, clean, clear smell. A beautiful flower with which to find harmony and comfort. It tells you that who you are running with may not be helping you to be in your totality.

Mint—Sometimes, when you can't remember clearly and there is a great shock or trauma in your life, it produces stimulation and increases your concentration. It reminds you that when life is full of work and no play, fatigue can be a doorway to death. It asks you to take time.

Morning glory—Secrets and special friends, talking, caring, and sharing.

Mum—Thinking deep thoughts, reading, remembering, and renewing your heart.

Orange—Speaks to you about self-confidence, about being conscious and aware of what is going on around you. It reminds you that life isn't all about yourself, but about reaching out and sharing with others.

Pansies—They weather the winter and stand strong in the summer, for they are solid. They speak of standing up for yourself and having self-esteem.

Patchouli—Protects you from things that go bump in the night and reminds you that even though we want to turn away and close our minds to what is evil, evil does exist. It asks you to attract the "good" in your life, and to find one who has the same awareness that you do.

Periwinkle—Calls you to a fresh, clean, new beginning, the loss of guilt.

Poinsettia—They invite you to a festive celebration, to connect and share.

Rose—Strengthens the inner being. It comes to you at a time of sadness and disappointment and asks you to rest and be calm, to understand that there are always reasons and there is always tomorrow. It brings about a gentle atmosphere.

Rosemary—When your ego is bruised, it opens a doorway of empathy. It helps you to improve your memory and to understand that the sun always comes out.

Sage—Speaks of ceremony and sacred honoring. It is an opening and cleansing, protective herb and plant.

Sandalwood—Is used to calm nervous tension. It soothes stress and brings about harmony. It enables you to study harder and asks you to look at things from all different points of view.

Tulips—They are the beginning. They speak of strong, new beginnings, strength, and simple life.

Yarrow—Speaks of marriage in the near future. It is time to listen and gather your energies. Yarrow is a true woman's plant that aids you in the beginning, in your young years of marriage, and helps you with menopause.

Wildflowers—They come to you and ask you to jump the line. They speak of freedom, color, and boundlessness. They say listen to the wind, for the spirits send messages from the spirit world.

MINERAL MEDICINES

Agate—Used to awaken one's talents. It brings about an understanding of self, strengthens the sight and diminishes thirst. It helps you to communicate with the spiritual purpose of your physical cellular structure. It promotes inspiration and connects your physical mind and the spiritual world.

Amethyst—A stone of pleasure and spirituality. It facilitates change, brings about moderation and the principles of metamorphosis, invigoration, and perfect peace.

Beryl—Instills guidance in all aspects of life. It enhances your physical individuality. Brings independence through thought and action.

Cat's Eye—Will give you great strength and luck. It will enhance your awareness and move unwanted energy from negative thoughts. Its protection energy helps you focus on having clear spiritual sight.

Chrysocolloa—Helps to produce stability in the body. It can help balance the blood sugar and strengthen muscular structure. It stimulates your crown chakra. It can be used to purify your home and environment. It promotes harmony, removes distress, and brings about great inner strength.

Citrine—A stabilizing stone used to balance your yin-yang energy. It also helps to align the chakras and ethereal planes.

Crystal—Known in many forms, it is quartz and is used for generating, promoting, enhancing, visioning, settling, calming, and intensifying your emotion. Solidifies your physicality, soothing and calming.

Granite—The stone of health. It is known to enhance purpose; it enables the attitudes of devotion, and helps to stabilize feelings of abandonment. It allows you to connect with your inner self and brings you energy.

Gold—Attracting the energy of physicality. It is used to obtain material substance and prosperity. It represents vanity and reflects the need for strong self-esteem.

Opal—Helps to invoke vision. It is a stone carried to enhance your ability to work with dreamtime. It is often known as a stone of happy dreams and changes. It can assist and help you become invisible in circumstances where you don't want to be noticed.

Peridot—Helps regulate cycles—physical, mental, and emotional. It provides a shield of protection for your body and can remove fear. It is a stone that helps the bruised ego. It helps you put yourself in order to move on to the next task.

Picture Jasper—A stone of universal, global, and world awareness, it promotes brother- and sisterhood and helps us to work with saving our planet.

Raw Ruby—Promotes connectedness, protection, clearing, and strengthening of the mind.

Sapphire—A stone of prosperity, it brings about focus and regulates energy, broadening your horizons. It is often shown in the form of a star, the closest thing to a star's presence in physical form. It promotes beauty and expands your mind to understand your beauty and intuition. It brings lightheartedness, joy, and a deepening of thought.

Silver—Allows you to be connected with Great Spirit, honoring and embracing. It gives you spiritual protection and strength.

SWIMMERS—FISH, REPTILES, MAMMALS

Alligator—Dangerous, rough, quick.
Dolphin—Playful, hope, bright.
Frog—Cheerful, happy, hope, renewal, clean.
Lizard—Daydreams, dreams, looking to tomorrow, illusions.
Salmon—Strategic, strong, wise, intentional.
Seal—Simple, organized, disciplined, plain.
Shark—Planned, cunning, treacherous, predator.
Snake—Transformation, change, growth.
Starfish—Magical, mystic, tranquility, calm.
Trout—Illusive, trickster, intelligent, spry, playful.
Turtle—Storyteller, keeper of knowledge, prosperity, fertility.
Whale—Knowledge, ancient knowing, solid, truth.

INDEX

To find out about conferences and workshops,
or to contact the author, visit our website:
www.wolfmoondanceauthor.com

Or write:
Wolf Moondance
453 East Wonderview Avenue
P.O. Box 6000
Estes Park, CO 80517

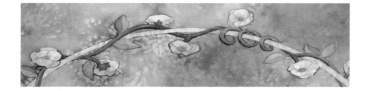